Dying Hard

Dying Hard

The Ravages of Industrial Carnage

Elliott Leyton

McClelland and Stewart

Reprinted 1975, 1977, 1979

ISBN 0-7710-5304-5

McClelland and Stewart Ltd.
The Canadian Publishers
25 Hollinger Road, Toronto

Manufactured in Canada
by Webcom Ltd.

For Bonnie

Contents

Foreword

This book is about dying miners whose bodies are ravaged by industrial disease and widows who have had to bear the consequences of their husbands' occupations. The book is academic in the sense that I use anthropological techniques such as the life history and participant-observation to elicit and present the material. But the book is not a piece of academic anthropology in the current "value-free" mode, and its aim is not an academic one.

My concern is to describe a national disaster in order to bring to international attention a problem which all industrial nations have studiously ignored throughout this century—their responsibility for industry-related disease, disability and death. It is my hope, perhaps a forlorn one, that this book will stimulate industrial nations to re-examine their obligation to the men whose bodies are destroyed in the process of creating wealth. To fail to do this is to admit moral bankruptcy.

This volume would never have appeared had not my Canadian teachers (especially Harry Hawthorn and R. W. Dunning) and my colleagues at Memorial (especially our Norwegian visitors, Ottar Brox, Georg Henriksen and Cato Wadel) stressed through example and argument the legitimacy of practical research. If anything can be said to distinguish Canadian social scientists from their colleagues in other parts of the English-speaking world, it is a commitment to the study of social reality. In this sense it can be said that this book contributes to a Canadian tradition.

This research would have taken intolerably long to appear had not Memorial University of Newfoundland and the Canada Council generously provided me with Sabbatical Leave. I am indebted, as usual, to Memorial's Institute of Social and Economic Research for many favours large and small, and to Miss Judy Bickford for her painstaking typing of the manuscript. I am grateful to many academics at Memorial and elsewhere who recognised the urgency of this enquiry; to David Alexander, Gordon Inglis, Robert Paine, Stuart Philpott and George Story for criticism and encouragement; and to John Jameson and Eric Leyland for freeing my energies.

But most of all I am indebted to the many people of the Newfoundland communities of St. Lawrence, Lawn, Lord's Cove, Lorries, Lamaline and Little St. Lawrence who took me into their homes and into their confidence. I owe a special debt to Des Jarvis and his family, true Lawners who nurtured my enquiry and my comfort in a hundred ways. Thirty men and women endured the pain of reliving their agony and relating the story of their lives: through the generosity of the Canada Council and the Institute of Social and Economic Research, I was able to offer each of them an honorarium as a token of respect. Through the efficiency of McClelland and Stewart, I am privileged to share any royalties this book may generate with the ten men and women whose stories are printed here.

In the preparation of this manuscript, not one word was added to the autobiographies. In their eloquence and in their tragedy they all possess that special quality the Irish call "a terrible beauty".

Elliott Leyton

1
The Carnage

Some one hundred men are dead[1] and another hundred await an early death in two adjacent villages on Newfoundland's foggy south coast. One household in every three has a dead or dying miner in the towns of St. Lawrence and Lawn. There is no family that has not been numbed by the loss of a father, an uncle, a son or a brother. Many have lost several.

The devastation of these communities was caused by industrial diseases contracted by the men working in St. Lawrence's fluorspar mines. Any man who worked steadily in the mines before 1960 (when Alcan took over the operation and installed ventilation) expects to die, is waiting to die. For the miners believe, not without justification, that eventually they will all fall victim to "the dust" and "the radiation"[2].

Silicosis and Lung Cancer are the primary pathologies induced by exposure to silica and radiation in the mine. But the physicians feel the mine conditions may be responsible for a much wider variety of diseases—including the range of obstructive pulmonary diseases (bronchitis, emphysema, pulmonary fibrosis and tuberculosis) and cancers of the bowel, stomach, bone, bladder and pancreas.

[1] Precise figures will never be known due to the unreliability of many earlier diagnoses. The estimate given here is a compromise figure.
[2] No one can state with certainty whether current health measures have eliminated, or merely ameliorated, the problem: only time will reveal that. In the meantime, however, new cases inexorably continue to appear among pre-1960 miners.

The miners, in their helplessness, will tell you that "no one knew". They are mistaken. Hippocrates observed some two thousand years ago that the metal digger is a man who breathes with difficulty. Agricola in 1557 recorded the breathing difficulty and observed that "when the dust is corrosive, it ulcerates the lung and produces consumption." In 1911, South Africa passed their first Compensation Act for Silicosis. In 1926, Rostoski, Saupe and Smorl completed their exhaustive clinical and pathological study of Saxony miners, more than half of whom died with cancer of the lung.

In 1937, when the first shaft was sunk and the holocaust began in St. Lawrence, medical science knew. They did not tell the miners. Mining engineers and government officials should have known; but no regulations of any kind restricted mining operations. This book documents the personal consequences of this indifference and neglect.

The Forces of Nature

When the last glacier left the St. Lawrence area less than ten thousand years ago, it left behind a land environment that was hostile and barren. Scraped of its soil by the glaciers and cooled by the icy Labrador current, it was little more than an extensive treeless bog dotted with innumerable small ponds. But the sea was rich. Rich in cod, rich in salmon and a host of other species. Europeans were quick to exploit the area once its wealth was known, and St. Lawrence became a summer fishing settlement by the late 16th Century.

Permanent settlement took place much later on this peninsula than in other parts of Newfoundland, but St. Lawrence was an established fishing settlement by the beginning of the 19th Century. Although the majority of the population were Irish and Roman Catholic, a large minority were of English Protestant origin: these latter, with no Church to marry or bury them, followed the pattern established elsewhere in Newfoundland—they converted to Catholicism and took on an "Irish" cultural identity.

Throughout the 19th Century and through the first quarter of the 20th, they worked in a traditional, small-scale, inshore fishery, dangerously vulnerable to swings in world cod stocks and market

12

prices. Their economic marginality earned them the appellation "slaves", and nowhere in Newfoundland was the feudal relationship between fisherman and merchant less rewarding than in St. Lawrence and its adjacent communities. With their poverty and their slavery came disease. Tuberculosis and malnutrition-related diseases devastated the settlements.

In 1929, even this fragile adaptation was smashed by two successive catastrophes. The crisis of international trade collapsed fish prices and left most families destitute. Then on November 18th, 1929, an earthquake off the Grand Banks sent three great tidal waves crashing along Newfoundland's south coast. The waves destroyed houses, boats and fishing gear. More important, they disturbed the codfish's feeding grounds. For four years the cod virtually disappeared. St. Lawrence and its sister communities were forced to turn en masse to the tender mercies of Relief.

In 1932, at the height of their desperation, a New Yorker named Walter E. Siebert arrived in St. Lawrence. In his book, *The Poverty Wall*, Ian Adams recreates the atmosphere surrounding Siebert's arrival:

> Siebert told the villagers that they were living beside one of the richest deposits of fluorspar in the world, that fluorspar was an essential ingredient in steel- and aluminium-smelting operations—why, if everyone turned to, in a couple of years St. Lawrence would have a booming industry. In March, 1933, a freighter arrived with a hold full of second-hand mining equipment. The men of St. Lawrence unloaded it without pay. The St. Lawrence Corporation was formed, with Siebert retaining full ownership and control, but the people of St. Lawrence were encouraged to think of it as "their mine". They believed in it.

The men of St. Lawrence went to work in "their mine"—to this day they still pronounce Corporation as "*Co-op*eration"—under conditions of extreme discomfort. No regulations of any kind governed the operations of the Company until 1951, and "many witnesses have testified that in those depression days a half-starved man was considered fortunate to hold a job where he could spend ten hours or so each day, drenched in the waters of Black Duck

13

Brook and half choked with dust from his 'hammer', trying to earn enough money to keep his family from starving, in an environment where fuel was just as scarce as food"[3].

Drilling was done exclusively with dry hammers which continually spew dust in the miner's face. In the words of one miner[4], the "hammer was hung on the shoulder which brought the drill hole directly opposite the driller's mouth. He at times used curtain scrim or cheese cloth over his mouth but this clogged in seconds and had to be discarded. Every few minutes he would have to shut off the machine to clear his eyes and nostrils of dust." At the time, however, the miners were unconcerned. They took pride in their ability to cope. And after all, "the dust was harmless."

In a way they were right. Fluorspar *is* harmless. But dry drilling in the host granite in the unventilated drifts released free particles of silica into the air which were then lodged in the miner's lungs. The lung's normal reaction to this invasion of foreign particles is a defensive one; the growth of healing scar tissue. This scar tissue begins to cover the lung and inhibits the cycle of gas exchange which is the function of the lung. As more particles are lodged, and more scar tissue grown, the lung's ability to "breathe" is progressively reduced. "The first symptom of silicosis is shortness of breath on exertion. Later the progressive massive fibrosis can and does cause disabling symptoms, leading to cor pulmonale and heart failure"[5].

Far worse, but undiscovered until the late 1960s, was the immense low-grade uranium deposit which backs onto St. Lawrence. Although the method of transmission has not yet been established, it seems that radioactive materials are brought into the mine "dissolved in waters which have percolated through joints and fractures of the granite. If inhaled, the charges they release rip up any body cells in their path, pictorially, like bolts of lightning striking a house"[6]. This irritant action causes the malignant tumour which is Lung Cancer, whose symptoms are progressive weakness, shortness of breath, cough, sputum, loss of appetite—and an early death.

[3] Royal Commission 1969, p. 33.
[4] Rennie Slaney, in Royal Commission 1969, p. 21.
[5] Royal Commission 1969, pp. 187-188.
[6] *Ibid.*, p. 53.

St. Lawrence and Lawn Today

At first sight, the two hardest-hit communities of St. Lawrence and Lawn look healthy, even charming. Clustered round their harbours, the water dotted with skiffs and dories, the settlements still have the character of fishing villages. The women keep the interiors of their tiny cottages exquisitely clean; men who are well ensure that the exteriors are in good repair, and friendly smiles wreath every face.

But one hundred men are dead and another hundred waiting to die. The grief and despair this generates takes place against a social background of community disharmony. A vital and egalitarian fishing society has been transformed into a Company Town with all its attendant uglinesses. Now a man's worth is measured neither by his kindness nor his wit, but by the "Co-operation's" infinite gradings of rank and salary. The snubbing of low-ranking wives by their "superiors", the farce of foremen everywhere flaunting their "boss's white hats" (even to bed, say some), and the extension of social privilege to company rank, create a heavy atmosphere indeed. This is exacerbated by what is to the miners the totally irrational and unfair manner in which Compensation is awarded and Welfare paid. Here, different sums of money are given to individuals according to medical and bureaucratic criteria which may make sense in the Board Rooms of St. John's, but which are utterly incomprehensible in St. Lawrence. Thus one miner is classified "30% disabled" and another "100%", and they are compensated accordingly. But in St. Lawrence, ruder functional categories apply. To be disabled is to be disabled—"you're either disabled or you're not." Similarly, one widow will receive a very large lump sum, while another will have her tiny stipend cut off entirely. These sources of perceived inequality create a social situation in which every man feels he is being treated unfairly. In the words of one elderly miner, "it's all begrudgement nowadays." A bitterness and distrust pervade the villages' affairs, persuade the dying that the world has gone mad, and fill their last remaining years with anxiety, confusion, humiliation and doubt.

When a miner first hears his death sentence from the local doctor, he tries to take it with stoicism. When the doctor first tells a miner, "I'm not too happy with your X-Ray, I'd like you to go up to St. John's and see a specialist," some men go white. Few ask anything about their illness: they do not wish to hear the details of their death sentence. Some men crack under the strain—"once you lose your nerve, you're gone." One man locked himself in his room for a day and a night; others pace the floor, pounding their fists and weeping. Others are so traumatised they wander in a deep depression, tears coming to their eyes when they realise this may be their last Christmas or their last summer on the pier watching the skiffs unload.

Meanwhile the Doctor calls in the miner's wife and sketches for her the clinical detail, trying to soften the blow with encouragement and optimism. Now she enters what in St. Lawrence and Lawn is virtually a separate status, that of impending widowhood. Now she must come to terms with her own intolerable future; the deterioration of his health, his drawn-out and agonizing death, and the grim prospect of raising the children who remain in her house —as many as twelve or fourteen—at the mercy of the Department of Social Assistance. Nor will her widowhood be buttressed by the support of the community, for the denuded kinship system of Newfoundland's south coast creates households which are largely isolated from one another. Those who remain are often too embarrassed to offer sustenance or aid; and some recoil from the widows —for in them, they see their own future.

When you first gaze into the men's faces, their countenances bear the calm and friendly expressions which Newfoundland culture dictates. But get to know one man, and see that the smile is forced; often on the lips, it is rarely in the eyes. Know one man very well and all you see is the fear, the loneliness, and the hurt from the disease that is greedily devouring his body. The penultimate blow to the dying miner is the loss of his sexuality. The miners believe that Silicosis destroys potency, a belief which is self-confirming. To spare individuals any embarrassment, I have removed accounts of this problem from the life histories in this volume. But it should be clear that even in this sensual culture the men must face their last days without the comfort of physical love. A quotation from one friend will suffice—

> Our foreman, he told me, "You know what that does with you? That'll even take away your nature. You won't want

women or nothing." And when I went to St. John's, that's the first thing the doctors asked me. And my nature has not been the bit the same as it used to be. Hardly any more than looking at that chesterfield. And he told me it done it with every one that died there. And that's the first frigging thing the doctor asked me when I went in St. John's, did I still have any nature? I said no, it was months, it must have been two or three months, never had a thing. And I'm like it today. Perhaps in months ne'er ever bother a woman.

Those who have received their death sentence watch each other with intense interest. They listen for the worsening of a cough, the gasping for breath and the vomiting. They watch for the collapse of the skin on the face, the hollowing of the eye sockets and the dulling of the eyes which presage the end of their suffering. On fine days when the atmosphere is sufficiently warm and dry that breathing is eased, the men emerge from their houses. Those with cars drive, those without begin the characteristic slow and jerky walk—stopping after ten or twenty steps to gasp for breath, then shuffling on again. Sometimes a walk of two hundred yards takes an hour, sometimes less than half an hour. It is painful to watch; excrutiating to share.

They gather on the fishing "stages" and in the "clubs", searching each other out. Leaning over the stage or over the club tables, the talk is of who is "failing", of who is in St. John's for treatment, of fights for Compensation and Welfare, of idle threats to "hang" the government officials who bring such unfairness to their lives. Linked by the intimate bonds of men who have lived together all their lives and now must soon die together, they compare their symptoms and assess the value of new treatment. If the news is of the death of one of their number, a fleeting smile followed quickly by embarrassment crosses a countenance here and there. Men in war experience the same—at first relief that it was someone else, and then a sense of shame for the all-too-human thought.

At the same time the men endure the combined ordeal of begging for Compensation and fighting off unwanted surgery that is so often part of their endless five-hundred-mile return journeys to St. John's. Humiliating themselves before the doctors and the Compensation Board to show how sick they are; fighting to avoid a "low" classification which would force them on to Welfare—a crushing indignity for those who have worked with pride all their lives; battling for lump sum payments large enough to repair their homes before they die; arguing against the treatment the St. John's doctors pressed upon them, the operations which seemed to kill every man who took them within months. Rarely are they told the results of any of their battles until weeks after they return home. Then they receive an impersonal note, typed perhaps by a young girl fresh from school who is paid more for her typing than the miner gets for dying, relating the bureaucratic decision.

Battles finally completed, the miners have the relative luxury of returning home to die. For some it is the mercy of a sudden heart failure. For more it is the slow deterioration of the body and its functions, the gasping and smothering, the lonely sleepless nights, and the final ordeal in terrible agony. Throughout this they know that when they go, no one will provide for their families with respect. There will be only the meagre allowance of Welfare, stunningly inadequate when there is no man to paint and repair, adjust and soothe. For many, the most heartbreaking loss is the loss of sociability, that special genius of Newfoundland culture—the activity around the stages, the endless lies about where the fish were caught, the ribald jokes and the teasing of the young men. This loss is most often symbolised by the inevitable forced sale of his dory on that terrible day when he can no longer climb aboard her.

Now the men wait. They listen to the messages their bodies send them—the breathing is getting harder, I can't walk to the car this year, I can't get over the side of the dory. As the choking and smothering intensify, the specially prepared bed stacked high with pillows so carefully stitched by their wives is rarely enough. To breathe through the night, some can only kneel over a chair sweating from the exertion of breathing and the fear that they will fall into too deep a sleep, go forward in the chair, and smother.

The pages which follow contain stories of true tragedy, of the fall from greatness. For those whose lives and impending deaths are described herein are no colourless ciphers. These pages tell the stories of Rum Runners and Sailors, Brawlers and Fishermen. Men who risked their lives to save hundreds of drowning sailors on their frozen beaches; men who slipped their rum-laden vessels past the machine guns of the U.S. Coast Guard and down the Hudson River; women who shouldered the crushing burden of widowhood with fierce courage.

All brought low by an enemy they could not see.

A Note on the Life Histories

Some thirty life histories were recorded on tape during the summer of 1974, ten of which were selected for printing here on the basis of their eloquence and depth.

Extended portions of each life history have been removed from this final version. This excision has been performed on various grounds which include the unnecessarily pejorative, the excessively personal (especially sexual material, or data on family quarrels), and the peripherality of the subject to our enquiry.

I have neither expertise nor special interest in the discipline of linguistics. But I have done my best to walk that line between removing the distinctive flavour of the Newfoundland dialect and reproducing an autobiography that would be incomprehensible to many English readers. In some cases I have used entirely arbitrary criteria in my decisions on the matter of spelling—sometimes reproducing exactly ("ahold to") and sometimes not ("thinking" instead of "thinkin' "). My decisions here were based on personal and aesthetic criteria alone.

While not one word has been added to the taped materials, I have felt entirely free to juggle paragraphs and sentences in order to clarify the autobiographies. This has been particularly necessary in matters of chronological progression, since most individuals abandon themselves to hopping between decades.

With the exception of several major figures, all personal names have been changed. Similarly, matters of place have been disguised, and I have altered some personal characteristics and descriptions in order to provide a degree of anonymity for my co-authors.

2

I was mucking,
I was drilling,
I was tramming

JACK CALLAGHAN: At 51, his once-vital face flattened by his body's trauma, Jack still exudes the sociability for which he is renowned.

I was born in Lawn. Me father was a fisherman, but me father died when I was eight years old. He got a chill in his arm back in the country, then he lost his arm and he died. We had nothing then, only poverty. When I was a child you don't know how bad it was. We used to get six cents a day, the whole family. Ground flour: time after time maggots'd be in that and you had to sift the maggot out of that or get it out the best you could. That was the worst that ever come around here was that maggoty flour. It was a poor grade of brown flour, the worst grade in the world it was that was sent around for the poor people. You'd open the sack and see it moving, moving.

You had to buy that with the six cents a day. Those steamers used to bring it here, and wherever you'd take up this little piece of paper and they'd name a merchant. You'd take it to this merchant, and that's all you could get was a bit of flour and a drop of molasses. There was no pork, no beef, no butter; only just if you had land and reared a cow you got a drop of milk from your own. Me mother used to get twelve dollars every three months after me father died, that was a pension, forty-eight dollars a year.

Although I never got no education I went to school a lot. Going to school late in the fall with bare feet. Not very much clothes either. Mostly then, it's just as well to be honest and tell the truth, they gather up flour bags and they'd make you a shirt or something like that. Get some dye and dye it and that was your rig then. No suits, no jackets, no sweaters.

I didn't have nothing when I got married in '45. I had to go and get the loan of the money to get married. It was very good, fish was picking up them years see and I got the money. It didn't take much money to get married, it was only twelve dollars. You had to give that to the priest to get married, twelve dollars. After I went in to the mine I stayed there. I had such a family, I got a family so quick, the kind of money you were making wasn't much good. It wasn't enough to keep them all going.

We had ground over there and we used to keep sheep and three or four cows. We'd sell one of them right late in the fall of the year, try to get a pair of boots for all hands. They didn't used to sell them around here at that time, they used to carry them in from St. Pierre. Stuff was cheap there. If you had older brothers, perhaps they'd be out partridging and they'd get a lot of partridges. They'd take them over to St. Pierre and sell them, perhaps two for twenty-five cents and they used to hook up a nice bit of stuff that way. They used to slip the partridges then. You used to go in the country, a big copse on the ridges, and you'd put down your stakes and you'd put your slip down between them. They'd go in and it'd go round their neck and you had them.

The Rangers was stationed in St. Lawrence. I was coming home this evening, I had sixteen or seventeen partridges. Cars was very scarce, there was only two cars on this neck around here and they belonged to St. Lawrence. I was coming down one side of Three Sticks and he was coming down the other side; I caught the glimpse of the car roof. I got in the copse, in the thick woods right around the road, and I hauled the nonny bag off me back. And he come right where I was at. He seen me just as quick as I see him. He called me by name, "Come out Bobby Winsor." So I had the bag off me back and I come out with the gun in me hand. He asked me what I was hiding for. I says, "I didn't think I was allowed to carry a gun": I knowed I was too. Well he must have kept me there about ten or fifteen minutes with the birds right alongside of the road. He asked me a few things, did I see Bobby? Well I never seen Bobby, so he went along. I walked almost home without me birds, I was afraid they'd come up and yard me. I went back and got the birds. But they never went a mile from that when they caught another fellow. They were after catching two that evening, just before that up here on our ridge. They caught me brother and another fellow. They give them fifteen days in jail. Yes, that's right, carried them off to Grand Bank and put them in jail. You weren't allowed to slip partridges see.

We used to have to get up and walk down to St. Lawrence. Sit around the Bank, wait to see the Relieving Officer. You'd be there all day. Perhaps you'd have to come home without nothing, he wouldn't give you anything. Next day you'd get up and go down again. And not very much to eat either. The people in St. Lawrence was the same way then, they didn't have it either, and you didn't know that many people. They were very nice, some people, they used to call you in and give you a cup of tea or whatever they had to give you, strengthen you up to get you home again. But we used to have to walk down there boy sometimes two or three times a week before they'd give it to you—for to get this Order, this six cents a day. Some days you'd go and he wouldn't give it to you. That was the Government style then; you weren't going to get it and come back tomorrow, they'd keep pawning you off. Many's the time I went down there and had to come back without it. And you'd go again and you'd go again before you got it.

Up until the time I got into the mine I had it pretty bad. Because fishing, the price wasn't that big, and you wouldn't getting all that fish. You had to go back to the Relieving Officer every week. So I got into the mine and that made everything a bit better. The money that I was getting wasn't meeting everything; not to feed them and try to repair your home too. I used to try to make a dollar every way I could. You'd come home and then go fishing. You had to break your day. Come in and get two or three hours sleep, you'd get up and get what fish you could and haul your gear in time to get back to work at four o'clock in the evening. Day shift you got a good bit of daylight left after you come home this time of year, you might be lucky to run out and strike a few fish.

They were all next to a bulldog because they had such strength and energy. They used to even row to St. Pierre, you know, that's thirty miles from here. All hands in the skiff had an oar apiece and they used to row, it was all day rowing. They used to carry over caplin. A good many used to do it. But I knows two men did it a couple times in a row dory. Me brother was one of them rowed to St. Pierre, with another fellow, a doryload of caplin. They used to get twenty-five cents a barrel, perhaps they carried eight or nine barrels, but if they went in skiffs they carried perhaps thirty-five or forty barrels. I know I was over one time with a load of caplin in a skiff and we got a dollar a barrel, so that was very good money. Goods was very cheap then. You'd buy sugar and tea and you'd buy tobacco and a drop of liquor, clothes. You always bought whatever you needed first. There was a warehouse where they stored the Gin caught fire one year, and they were selling it a dollar a case, a dollar for twelve bottles. There was some Gin brought out of St. Pierre that year. It was number one Gin.

From 1929 up until the latter part of the Thirties there was nothing. The tidal wave cleaned her. Never left a thing on this coast. They started coming back in the Forties, there was lots of fish then. Them fellows were at it then, they only used to be out once or twice a day, but God they couldn't clear their traps then. And then everybody started coming back to the fishery again. Now last year it wasn't that big a voyage but it was very good. But a few years before that they had some wonderful voyages; two or three skiffs landed as high as fourteen, fifteen hundred thousand each, and the lowest boat around was three hundred thousand. Prices were low, you weren't getting no money for it. We started selling it first we used to get fifteen dollars a thousand pounds, and then she used to go up a dollar a year. The one little plant there in Burin couldn't handle it, there was so much fish up and down the shore, and they had draggers of their own. Every one would be loaded, dories and skiffs, waiting to try to get clear of them. Wait all day and then have to come back and split what you could, the plant wasn't able to take it. Because the longer they'd be laying, they'd be getting soft.

There was only a few ever went away. Because at that time you couldn't go nowhere. You had to have money to go. You weren't allowed in Canada, you had to go through an Immigration they call it and you had to have money enough where you were able to look after yourself and come home if you couldn't get work.

Because the Government wouldn't have nothing to do with you. And there wasn't many people had that much money. And then when you're coming back you couldn't bring nothing back with you, it'd be all took away from you in Port-aux-Basques, you had to go through the Customs. You could bring money, but you couldn't buy anything and bring it into Newfoundland then. Not until we got into Confederation. It was the first time ever you were allowed back and forth to Canada. You couldn't get out of Newfoundland, because the States was the same thing. Anyone that had lots of money didn't want to go. I was going to go one time and I give it up, never went. After I got married I never bothered going anywhere. A lot of people in the Forties after the war broke out went over to the Forestry in Scotland, a whole lot went from here, cutting wood and timber. Two or three stayed over there. They made good money over there.

First time I ever went in to Salt Cove Brook, I went in there on the surface in '40. Worked a few months on the surface and then I went underground. I worked so long, and then come home for a spell fishing, and then back again for another spell working. I boarded there for a spell, thirteen months, but I never lived there. We used to shack there, camp ourselves where the mine was at. The Company had shacks made there, about six or seven people in it, bunks alongside of her, a table and a stove. Carry your own grub, cook for yourself. And then after a spell the Company put a cookhouse there. You paid. Five that were in my shack are dead. They all had the miner's disease.

When I went down there first boy we started off on the one hundred and fifty foot. The drift was only narrow, just room enough to shove a little trolley and track, about two foot wide I suppose. Just shove your trolley up to the face, and you used to have to fire back the muck to your mucker with a hand shovel. You'd load up and come out and dump it down into a bend. The bucket'd come down and somebody'd load it and hoist it up. It was good there then because she wasn't mined out. You had a little drift, only six feet or eight feet wide, and the ground wasn't hurted that much. Only just cutting a path through. And then after we sunk another shaft, we started *mining* there then. Driving stopes here, there and everywhere, thirty, forty feet wide. Well everything got pretty shattery. Lots of humps you looking up at, you never knows if they was going to stay up there.

In the first eight or ten years they done a cruel lot of dry drilling. No water see. They were only using a dry hammer and there was nothing, only smoke and dust all the time. Well that going down into your throat all day long had to go somewhere. You were all the time blasting, you couldn't hardly live with the smoke down there then, there wasn't that much air see. It used to bother you, but you had to try to do the best you could. You'd just draw back for a spell till she'd blow out a bit. You'd turn on your air hose and blow out your drift as clear as you could get it, you'd clear away your chutes, and start mucking again. When you were going ahead with your light, you could see something like a fog, your light was shining through streaks. You'd see circles, you often see the sun shining like that. Outside of that boy she was a beautiful spot to work.

Safety? All I ever heard when I was there was there an Inspector or anything coming, start cleaning up and barring off crossways, manways and everything. About a month before they were coming, the Company knows they were coming. And everybody was working and cleaning it up and having it just right for them to look at. The Government give the Company a chance I suppose. You're in there days and days cleaning up the track and having it right perfect. Taking away all the old timber and hoisting it up, picking up all the loose dynamite because everywhere you looked there'd be dynamite here and there. Get all that picked up and packed away.

I was mucking, I was drilling, I was tramming. I was at it all when I was there. I liked the mine good when I was there. The reason why everybody did like it was you went down there and the time used to go wonderful fast. Say if you had a contract, perhaps fifty buckets. Well if you got good going, you got that in a couple of hours with a trammer hauling ten buckets at a time. You always made it in four. And then you had the other four hours home. She was good that way. Although we were getting no money we were getting a lot of breaks. It was a very good spot to work. They'd give you a job, and you had to do your best. And if you didn't get it all every time you went there, they didn't throw any sauce at

25

you. They were pretty fair that way. But you had something to do and you went down. You were always two or three of you together, you worked in and made the best of it you could for the next shift coming on, have it cleaned up for them. We used to have to get fifteen buckets for the Company, and then after that you'd get ten or fifteen cents for yourself for a ton bucket.

After *it* come out there was a lot of disagreeing, a lot of talk. Because they really should have been let know. If the Company knew it, the Doctors knew it, it really should have been let out before it was. If it was in those other big mines up in Canada it was kept very quiet and nobody knew nothing about it. Then there was a lot of people talking about it, a whole lot of people. The Company wouldn't do nothing for them after anyhow, because I suppose it was throw you over to the Government. They paid you for what you done was the way they looked at it. I was working with them and they could say, "Well, I paid you; I never have to keep you no more."

When I found out the radiation was in the mine, I jumped ship, got out. There was times boy you wasn't feeling that good. You were short breathed, and lots of times you were there when you shouldn't be there. And then the pay was so low, if you lost a shift it was almost the same as you lost the whole pay. You didn't want to get fired, eh? You had to try to get there if you was feeling well or if you wasn't feeling well. Say you didn't go down today, tomorrow I'd go down and they'd send me to the Doctor for a Paper. Well that's two shifts gone. You couldn't really afford to do that.

When the Doctor come out and told about the radiation, it leaked out. Dr. Quinlan, he come to the meeting and he told us what was there. The Union got to call the people together in the Hall. He explained see what we were up against. He come out and he told us, "You were working in radiation, and one hour is as good as one year." The way he explained it, the weakest part of your system, no matter what part of your body that was, that was the part this thing would hit. Whether it was your lungs, chest, head, legs, whatever the weakest part of you was.

I never even went back looking for a job on the surface after I come up, because I didn't want any more to do with them. I thought I might be after escaping it. And to hell with it, because I knowed they were after testing everything then and the mill was reading just as much as underground. So I suppose all over the place it was, wherever the 'spar was at. The whole air was full of it. Fellows that never went under the collar got it, so goddamnit, they had to get it somewhere.

They're after dying just the same as he says. Sam O'Reilly, I worked with him three years, the two of us together. And so help me God I didn't know him. That's where he got it, in the eyes. After they told me that's who it was, I wouldn't believe it. If anyone shot me, I'd say "no, that wasn't Sam O'Reilly." He was raised out; by God, it went right to his brain.

I can remember sitting down in our Hall playing Bingo one night with a man that I worked with for years. There was hardly any difference in him to look at him than you. And all of a sudden he got a little bit queer and no time after he was feeling miserable. Jesus, he never lived not three months. He got operated on and gone as quick as that. They opens you up and it fills you full of air. I think pretty well the first person from St. Lawrence to go in to take the operation was Alistair Andrews. He come back with the lungs took out and told everybody he was sound cured, and in a couple weeks he was going to go fishing or go back to work. He came here one day looking for a lobster and he told me he was feeling pretty miserable. A couple weeks after that he was in there then, gasping for breath. Never laid an eye on him after.

Before the Doctor let it out, in the latter part of '59, I'd been off a few months and I wanted to go to work again. Our foreman, Murdock Justin—God Almighty couldn't make them any better than that, we all loved him—he told me this in his own kitchen. He said, "You're not going back there again." And I says, "Yes boy, I'm going back there again." He said, "You knows what's down there, don't you?" And I says, "No, I don't." "Well," he said, "they're dying down there." And everything that he told me is after happening too. He said, "You know what that does with you what's down there? That'll even take away your nature, you won't want women or nothing. That's a fact." So it was a funny sickness isn't it? It goes through your whole system I suppose. But I didn't believe him. I thought he was figuring he didn't want to take me back.

The year Alice was born, '67, I went down to the Doctor. I was feeling miserable. I was on the Relief, the "punky" they used to call it. We was waiting for the Relieving Officer to come to get the Order. I was drawing twenty-three dollars a week. So this day the Relieving Officer comes and tells us we had to go to Burin to work in the fish plant. There was going to be no more Relief. You had to go get a medical. So I went down to get a medical. A week was up and I had to go back for a report. So I gets in to Dr. Hollywood, and Jesus, he was frightened to death. I said, "I'm supposed to get a medical to go to work." "Lord," he says, "you're not going to work, you're going home." He sat down to the desk and wrote a letter, put in it an envelope, and said, "You get home now and get this off to the Welfare Officer as fast as you can." About a month after that we gets the Social Assistance then, turned down. Not too long after that I gets a call to go in to St. John's. So I went up to Dr. Wilder and he goes all over me and everything and told me me chest was rotten, "You had a cruel bad chest." So he give me another Paper and I had to go to General Hospital for some more tests. The Doctor he say he wanted an operation. So I told him, "No, I'm not taking no operation." I suppose they must have got fed up on me then, so they sent me home. They wouldn't give me the money, but it was a good spell before they bothered me anymore.

In April they called me back to the Confederation Building. Three Doctors there then, Dr. Stewart, Dr. Wells and Dr. Sullivan. Lord Jesus, one fellow got me in there and he went all over me, twisting and turning and drawing. He went out and the other fellow come in, and he done the same. Then the other fellow come in and he done the same. If they hadn't knocked off I would have fallen on the floor because it was too much. I wasn't feeling that well, and they were forcing you.

Put me clothes on and the Doctor took me down to this great big board. "There's your X-Ray," he said, "there's all evidence of silicosis there. But we got to have a piece of your lung to have the real proof." "You're not getting no piece of my lung," I said. "Well sir," he said, "the proof is there, you got it; but we can't do nothing for you till we gets the real proof." He wanted a piece. Dr. Wells there, he said, "You know Mr. Callaghan, we got to have proof before we can give you Compensation." I said, "Well you're not getting no piece of my lung! Everyone ye cut, do you know where they're at? They're in the graveyard." But he said, "Today we got all new equipment and everything, the latest." I said, "They're not made yet that's going to cut me." He said, "How much would you get in a year on Compensation?" The other fellow said, "He'd get between six and seven thousand dollars a year." That was more or less to try to buy you over. They were offering you that much money. I said, "No, I'm going to live on what I'm getting." He said, "How much are you getting?" Three hundred and fifty dollars on the Social. He said, "I'll tell you what we'll do. You go home; and if they takes the Social away from you, we'll give your Compensation." That's the words he said to me, so help me God!

I knows men that worked there twenty years that they never give nothing to. What's better than that, he told me that he come off Sick Leave, and after he got his Compensation, begod they tried to take it back. The Company tried to take back the Sick Leave they were after giving him. I think Christmas they sent him out a ten dollar bill. So I mean they didn't do very much for nobody. They wouldn't give you a cent. I knows a man now was sent up this year. He was took up from underground, he had to get up. He tried to stay down as long as he could, but directly they come and said you got to get up. He went up to the Doctor. All he got was his wages and his holiday pay, and go to work on the surface if he wanted to. Now that was in the middle of the winter, in February that was. Now to take a man up from somewhere it's warm, stick him out in the frostiest kind of weather! Now he had to be sick to be drove up didn't he, so why try to put him out somewhere and freeze him to death in another few months? There was a good many of them got surface jobs after they come up out of it, but they were gone in a few months or a year.

Frank Ryan, he was sent into St. John's the early fall, and he got his Compensation, he got $2,800 back time. I don't know what his monthly salary was, but according to what his lump sum was it couldn't have been more than fifty, sixty dollars a month. And as soon as he died, they cut his wife off right away. She never got a cent since. I don't know how that happened, because there's another woman over there, her husband died and she still gets it.

They gets right dirty with you too now in there, the Doctors and the Nurses. Someone told me when Frank Doran was in there, they were very quare with him. One of the nurses said to him,

"You're like everyone else comes in from out there, you don't want to take nothing." Well I figure that'd be up to a person's self. Eh? They wanted Frank to take the operation too, and I think they were very disappointed with him. The way they spoke to him, they didn't want to see him anymore because he didn't go up and take an operation. And they had another fellow dressed for an operation—and there was a fellow from here in the same room, Bob McGrath—and they were getting him ready to cart up to the operation. He said, "Where you going with me?" "We're going to operate on you." "No," he said, "there's nobody operating on me." Well he had a big row and he cleared out that evening. So they were just going to take that on their own.

They thought sure to get to operate on me. The Little Devil I called him, that was his name, Dr. Mack. He took me over to the Board. That was very, very selfish for a man to take you over and show you your own disease. "There it is," he says, "there's all evidence of Silicosis. We got to have the real proof, a piece of your lung." In the neck they cuts you and gets a piece of you. They could have said, "Well boy, go on home, we'll send you your cheque." What was mine was mine.

Whatever year I got it, I gets a call to go out to the Compensation Board. I was up before the Board so long. And all that Doctor done with me the next morning; I went up and just hauled off me shirt, he went around me chest and back and forth over me back, that was all. And two weeks after that I had me money, $6,700. And all before that they wanted to operate, operate. To do away with you, that's all they wanted to do, I'm just as sure as God in Heaven. I suppose there's big money for them for operating; and they learn more about those things, cutting you open and just sewing you up again. The fellow was in with me that time, Paul Connell, they tried to do the same with him at that time. Well we were talking back and forth and he refused it that time. But he was no time home when he went in and took this operation, and it wasn't three months after that he was dead. And his own brother told me he didn't know him when they brought him home that day. He was gone so far he melted right out of the world.

Me son, anyone's got that and he takes the operation, just like that! Jack Malraux went in there and he come home, they were supposed to have him cured. He wasn't a man, he was a giant.

Jesus, I think you'd have to hit the man in the head with a mawl to kill him. He went in less than three months. Not one of them lived. The only one that did live to three months was Alistair Andrews. Another fellow, he used to live right here, they operated on him and we said to him, "In a month now boy, you'll be fishing." Jesus, in a month we were burying him. It was fine for them, they were trying to learn something about this. There's nobody got any cure for it, it'll never be cured. But it wasn't good for the fellows getting the operation.

I'm not feeling all that good. I'm uneasy about that frigging heart. You see I had a brother died with heart trouble, he went just like that, never even got time to speak to no one. You never feels good after the heart attack, you've always got pains down through your shoulder and in your back and your breast. I ne'er ever thought I had anything wrong with me heart.

That was a young fellow that was some sick was Ron Sullivan. Me Jesus, he was some bad. He used to go right black. What a cough he had. I got something the Doctor give me; you put it in your mouth and press on the button, something will squirt down your throat and bring back your breath. But he never got to make that that morning. He couldn't reach it, it took him too heavy. He never got to reach out to get his blower. He went off.

It's very grim. I got no good hopes at all. I feels too miserable mostly, sometimes I feel so frigging miserable. I'll tell you you're having a lot of colds and everything, it really gets you down at times. You go out and do any little thing at all and you'll come up with the flu. And me chest is not all that good.

And me breath is getting shorter. A lot shorter. I used to cough, me Jesus I'd cough half the night. I'd have to pillow meself up for to get to breathe. I used to choke. The night is the worst. Oh me son, I had some bad nights. This treatment after I had the heart attack, I'm really finding that keeping me chest and tubes a bit clearer. I'm taking eighteen pills a day. One is a little nerve pill. Dr. Hollywood told me, "You're cruel a-quiver." I mean twasn't me, it was whatever was inside me doing it. I suppose when the lungs start to go it's got to be bearing on something else. It's like an engine; when one thing wears, something else wears. Jesus, I was ridiculous with the cough, I was almost ashamed to go any-where. Cough, cough, cough, cough, I used to have so high as two and three hours steady coughing at night, honest to God. And I'd get the pillows and try to rise meself up. That's what used to have me up so early every morning, I used to get up because I didn't want all the youngsters woke up.

That's the way of it boy. It gets a little worse. It got to get worse, it's not getting better. Like Hollywood told me, "You only can expect one thing, that it's not going to get no better." He told me mine was holding its own, it's holding pretty good. There's only one thing you can live for—to live as long as you can.

3

Shortness of breath, that's the first thing

PAT SULLIVAN: perhaps the oldest miner in St. Lawrence, he owes his longevity to his late start in mining. Celebrated for his indifference to pain, he has sewn together deep gashes in his own body. Both he and his son are dying.

I used to eat everything. Anything that I could pick up I could eat. Any kind of insect. Makes no difference what it was. Caplin, live caplin, squids, all that kind of stuff. I often went down to the dock with squids running ashore, take up the live squid and tear him abroad, chew him up and eat away just the same as having Coke. And the caplin the very same thing. And any kind of insect, butterfly, or them big flies; take them up and eat away at them all the time. And I have took the guts out of a squid nine days old—you know what they were—and put them between two slices of bread and butter and eat away. Just for devilment that's all, just for badness.

We used to be working up in Number 3 there; those big caterpillars they calls them, they're bigger than butterflies. At night they'd be stuck around the head frame, around the light, hundreds of them. I'd go up and get me ten or fifteen of them, bring them in and squat them up between the bread, sit down and eat away at it. That's really true now, I'm not telling you no lie there because anyone at all around here now can tell you. Three parts of the crew working there, they wouldn't touch a bit to eat. It never turned me. You would be able to do the same thing. But if you looked at it, you wouldn't be able to eat that.

All me family was the same as that, the whole works. Me poor old father now, warbles in cattle, he used to put his thumb down inside them, squat them out, put them in his mouth, chew them up and eat away. In the hide, a kind of a bug, they're about as big around as your thumb, right coal black they were. Everything. Any kind of insect. You often sees them on the road there, in the grass, black ones. You went along and perhaps you'd tread on them, he'd take them up in his mouth and eat away at them. And he lived to be eighty-four, me poor old father, never had a doctor in his life, never had a pain nor an ache. He went fishing in a dory here when he was eighty-two, cross-handed. And when he was eighty-four, he sat up in the bed and died. Never had a pain nor an ache.

I was only nine months old when me mother died. I had sisters then, me oldest sister was about sixteen. She died there now last fall, eighty-seven she was. And she had three strokes before she died, and she got the better of the three and cured herself. Never went to no doctor or nothing. She cured herself with the Sloan's Liniment, three times a day rubbed. She took a stroke there last fall and went on just as quick as that.

I was eleven year old when I went to go fishing. I fished with Mr. Beck along up the harbour, he's dead and gone now. I was down on the beach, a little boy in me bare feet pitching buttons, five or six of us. He come along then and he said, "What are you at, Pat?" And I said, "Pitching buttons, sir." He said, "What about a shipman, I'm looking for a young fellow to go fishing." I said, "Yuh, all right." "Go up and ask your old man," he said. I come up and said, "Old man, Mr. Beck down there wants me to go fishing." He said, "What the devil you want to go fishing for? You're no good to go fishing." I said, "I'm going to go anyway." He stopped for a little and I said, "What for, can I go?" "All right," he said, "if you thinks you're all right, go on."

Well, I went up to the hardware then. You got thirty dollars a month and your grub and a suit of clothes and a pair of boots. Now you started to get little boots then, they'd come up to about there and they had a red ring around them. So I got the oil clothes and the boots, and his wife gave me a pair of socks, so I put the boots on. I had a piece of rag in me pocket, and when I come down the harbour with me boots on, every time I tread on a pothole, I'd kneel down and brush the mud off. That's what I thought about a pair of boots then.

Me dear sonny boy, the times was hard. We used to get Relief from the Government, what they calls Able Bodied Relief. You know what we used to get then? A pickle bottle full of molasses for a week. That was a very small drop. You'd get so much tea then, so much flour and so much barley. And the barley'd be right coal black, just the same as mice dirt it was. That's what we used to eat them times. A very small lot for a meal. Many's the time I got up in the morning, going into the woods, take a crust of bread burnt coal black on the stove and take a drop of tea. Hard enough.

I went trapping after that, fishing with the Farrells. You'd get a half share then; when you're so young you could only get half a share. Then when you'd get up to man's age you'd get a full share. I was with Farrell about ten years I guess, trapping. Then I used to go up winter time for them, tending cattle. They had a lot of cattle, sheep, horses, hens, all kinds of stuff. Thirty dollars a month and your grub they used to give. I used to go up there in October and I'd be there till April, in a shack about five miles in. If food'd run out, you'd come out and get more. Then I spent five more year after that up there with old Mr. Giovannini tending cattle. Get up in the morning, light the fire, sluice the stables, milk the cows. By Christ, do it all.

I'd be fishing seven or eight year, we'd be on the draggers winter time. I'd be in Halifax, Sydney, knocking around. When I was in Halifax I used to be working in the sugar refinery—every fall you'd pretty well go, eh? That was one thing, there was no trouble getting work in those time. Best kind of a job. Me son, if you'd ever seen the deck you'd never eat another bit of sugar. The sugar brought in was dumped out on a great big pile, and they used to haul it in with the horses at that time and dump it out, and the horses' manure among that, all kinds of dirt. But once that goes through the refinery, everything was gone right to powder. I used to be bagging, bagging it up. That was in the Twenties. You enjoyed your life. Jesus it was all kinds of fun. Night time you'd be up at the Sailor's Institute, there'd be all kinds of records, playing all kinds of games and everything like that. You'd be home in the summer time to fish, and in the fall of the year you'd go away.

The first wife died in childbirth, she was thirty-three years of age. I had the second wife here housekeeping three year before I married her. Her husband and his brother too, the two of them was drowned, looking for their herring nets in the winter time. A storm come on. They was never seen or heard tell of afterwards. They picked up the dory and that was all. I'll tell you how I met her now. Couple fellows working there in Number 3 with me belonged to Fortune Bay, and I had nobody, nobody to look after me after the woman died. So one fellow says to me when we're sat down and having a few drinks, "Uncle Pat," he says, "I can get a housekeeper if you wants one." "Yes boy, if you can get one, right enough." So that's how it come across. She kept house for three year then, and after that we got married.

I was nineteen year working underground. The mine here, that was on the go about fifty year before Siebert come down here to go to work. They used to come and stake land, marking off their claims. Finally then they come here and staked it all out. They had to come back again and open it up. That's where they opened, the old Black Duck in there. We started in there, that's what we used to get an hour, twenty-eight cents for drilling. We worked with pick and shovels, it was all pick and shovel work, we had no power see. Used to have to work with a bean can—weren't much fruit cans on the go them times—used to have the candle in inside for our light. Then by and by the carbide lights come in.

And then we had to dig them a trench on the outside part of the mine. It took us three weeks to do that, we done that on "protest" —if it turned out any good we'd get paid, if it didn't turn out no good we didn't get paid at all. When we got inside there, if you found ore all right you'd get paid for it, if you didn't find ore, well you didn't get paid for it. We done lots of free work. We done the tunnel in there to Salt Cove Brook, to dig down see was the vein of ore there. As it happened, we dug down about twelve feet and struck the ore.

Jesus, Mary and Joseph, there was no conditions then. We worked down at Iron Springs, we had an old shaft there with thirty, forty steel barrels; well that's where you'd go in to have your lunch, on that. And no toilet, nothing at all. Stormy night now you wanted to do your business, you'd go out and dig a hole in the snow out in the woods, your clothes down around you. You'd be drifted in lots of times. We started working, we had one suit of oil clothes for the three shifts. Say I went in at eight o'clock in the morning, well I'd put it on and go down. You'd come on at four o'clock, I'd take it off and you'd put it on. Same way at twelve o'clock at night.

And then we started to sink a shaft in the west end of Black Duck. Me and Bill Rose, he died here not long ago, and another fellow, we spent three weeks at that. And Lord, do you want to know what we used to do with that? There was three of us and we had a two-gallon bucket, and that way we used to try to keep the water out, with that. I'd top it up and hand it to poor old Bill Rose, Rose'd hand it up to the other fellow, and he'd heave it out of the mine. We spent three weeks and never got nowhere at all. And then we brought in a pump, one of those hand pumps. And you had to pump at that! Your mug up (lunch), you had to lay it down on its side so you could reach and take the bread and shove it in your mouth. If you knocked off pumping a minute, perhaps it'd be three hours before you'd get it dry again.

Dust? Jesus, dust. Once you got down and closed in and started driving a drift down underneath, you'd go in Sunday night twelve o'clock. Everything'd be right bright, just the same as here in the house. Four o'clock in the morning then you'd have a round drilled off, you'd fire the dynamite. That'd be all. No more. You'd just glimmer the bulb like a match all the rest of the week. It'd turn right red with the dust and smoke.

I was firing there when we had a fellow killed. That's the first fellow that ever was killed there. He was killed through his own fault in one sense of the word. I was shot firing. We had fifteen shots in. When he started to come out, there was a shot there that wouldn't burn. If that shot didn't go, the rest of the shots would be spoiled, because that's the one that had to bust up the underpart. Then he stopped. Aloysius Andrews said, "Come on, we're going to be caught with that if you don't come out of that." Aloysius, he took his light and went on. I hung on and hung on, only I said, "Neddy me son, come on, you're gone too long now, that's going to go directly." So I started to come back. And I was just around the turn when bang she goes. I knowed then he was killed. After the smoke cleared away, me and Aloysius Andrews went in. We walked in over him when we went in. We searched round; he was wearing a pair of those XL rubbers, white on the toe. And Aloysius sung out, "Christ, come here, he's killed!" That's what was showing over the muck, the XL rubbers.

There was five or six killed at Salt Cove Brook, and two down in Iron Spring. But there's not too many for what work went on there. Sperrin, he was killed there. There was a slab hanging out of the wall, it should have been took out a long time before that, people was talking about it. Sperrin was down there mucking away when down come the slab. Brought the head right together.

And we had another man killed there, Mr. Watkins. He was repairing the shaft. The bell rung and the fellow what was on the hoist, he hoist the bucket. Old Mr. Watkins went on right down about a hundred and twenty feet I allow, when he struck on a piece of two by six, a plank what went across the shaft. And he broke that. The fellow what was on the hoist, he's been in the Mental ever since. He blamed hisself for killing him. And the people even went to him and told him; the boys belonging to this man went to him and told him, "Don't you blame yourself." "Oh yes," he said, "I killed him." He got so damned bad he used to lock hisself up in the house, be up all night long. So one night he got clear, and he had one of those straight razors, and he got up in the barn. They missed him. Begod they went after him. They figured that's where he went, the barn, and when they went to the barn he had his throat cut. The blood was going everywhere. So they took him and carried him to the doctor, got him fixed up. He wears a scarf so you won't see the cut, right across the throat that is. He's still in the Mental. He'll never come this way no more.

It must be eight or ten year before they started to complain. Shortness of breath, that's the first thing. That was the trouble first. Poor Jack O'Brien was the first what felt the choking, the smothering, gasping for breath. After that then everybody used to get it. You'd get gassed, they used to have to hoist you up, just the same as you were dead. Get up on the snow and pant, pant, pant, gasping for breath. Me Jesus, Mary and Joseph, I passed out about fifty times. Fifty times they had to hoist me up. There'd be fellows you had to hoist up every day. You'd be down there working, and it'd be just the same as you're getting drunk. You're getting right groggy and you stagger. I got so bad there one day; when you got so far gone the only thing you could do was lie right down on the bottom of the mine and put your face right down in the water. If you didn't, you wouldn't come to; you'd have to smother, that'd be it. Gas does it see. Wasn't only me, lots of fellows like that. They'd hoist you up. Sick! Lord Jesus, vomiting! Me son, you'd vomit and you'd be all right then. But a headache; not a headache like you'd have, but it was going just the same as a horse galloping. Jesus. Then you'd go back to work again. You always had the headache, the dynamite do that. All the time you worked you had the headache, everybody.

We were up in Number 3 drilling one day, and we were drilling out the muck. We were going to put a deck in. So we cleared it all away, scaled it all down, and I said to them, "I think that's pretty safe there." And they said, "Yes boy, there's nothing there to hurt now." So they started drilling. That was about nine o'clock I suppose. Poor old Josh, he was the general foreman, he come down at about ten o'clock to where we were at. When he come in outside a pile of muck, he stopped and he looked. I don't know what he seen, he must a seen the ground shivering. So he said to them, "Boys, you'd better get back out of that, that don't look too good in my eyes, that don't there." He said, "Come out here and we'll have a smoke." So we all went back there and we never had a cigarette half smoked out when Jesus, me son, down she come. The rock right give out. The rock, the sod, the water, the mud, the wood, the whole shagging thing come down. The muck! Six days a mucking out of that. And that jackhammer, the hose, was all in under that. Some wonderful things happened people got clear of, I'll tell you that.

We drove the drift up there sixteen hundred and sixty feet; jack-hammers and not a drop of water. Your drills would get smothered and then you'd knock off; and you had to hook your nose out to get to breathe, you'd be choking so much. And cough up when you're up and spit on the snow, just the same as you're coughing up blood.

I hung out for a long, long time, boy. That was before I started feeling too bad. Used to be miserable all the time before I got right down. The last two year I worked, that's when it struck me. The first few years you'd lose the use of your legs; you'd be going, going, keep going and you wouldn't know nothing till they were gone. The last couple years I worked you used to die with that coughing, twenty times a day. You'd come up and get the air then. After you'd get the air, perhaps you'd be all right another hour, couple of hours. Then it'd take you again. I'd say I worked sixteen year before it took any effect on me. I worked nineteen year altogether. Sure I knowed. You knowed what was the matter then, you knowed what was wrong with you. I quit the mine in '52. I couldn't do it, couldn't get up and down the mine, because we used to have to walk up and down the mine.

I think poor Joe Callaghan died the hardest death. He was forty-two days and forty-two nights and never took a bit of nothing, only a drink of cold water. Me Jesus, Mary and Joseph, he died hard. If you knowed him and seen him after he died you'd say you never saw him before in your life. And poor old Isaac O'Reilly over there, a great big robust two hundred and eighty pounds. Oh my, he died ninety pounds. He was nothing only the bone. And he'd go down the beach, he had a truck then, and I said what the hell you doing down here Isaac? And he said, "I got to stop down here till the crew's done with dinner and cleared away. If I goes home now, as soon as I smells the food, that's it, I'm gone." Vomited his blood up.

Me son Theo, oh boy he's sick. He's really sick, that man. Mostly what's the matter with Theo is Arthritis—it's gone through the bones—and Silicosis and Cancer. Last time he was in to the hospital he signed hisself out of the hospital. The doctor started exercising him in the morning and he couldn't stand the pain. Buckle his legs out, then straighten him out. He'd crack and he'd screech, you'd hear him all over the hospital. "Doctor," he said, "I can't stand that no longer. Give me me clothes, I'm getting out," he said. So he come on home. And he went on a drunk, by God he was on a drunk three or four days. Then his birthday come the 26th, he started up again. I take up and carted him off to hospital. He went down and took a pain in his chest. I thought he was gone that evening.

The doctor and one of the janitors took him and carted him upstairs. If Theo sets down on the bed he can't get up. No, he can't get up. One gets on each side of him and helps him get up, he's all right then, he can go. He's not all right; he can't walk anyway. He'll get up about twenty times, half way up. He's some pitiful. He's a pitiful man.

All the time in pain. Never slacks off at all because it's in the bones. He's got Cancer of the Bowel; the blood runs with that just the same as the water, down through his backside the same as the water. He takes the cramps in the stomach, he's mostly always got the cramps—Diarrhoea goes with the Silicosis. If you go in and look at it afterwards, it's just the same as you killed an ox, right blood red. All his insides is after being saturated with blood.

He's putting up a hard time of it, he is boy. Pain in his bowels, right across there, and up his chest. He can't breathe at all, for he's smothering all the time he is. All the bones, every bone that's in him is full of Arthritis. If you ever gets Arthritis in your bones, say you got it in your shoulders, you'll screech like a lamb. Oh me Jesus, Mary and Joseph he does. And you go down there and one of you take a hold on him each side to let him up and you'll hear him down on Dock Street next, the pain. He takes pills all right. They don't do you no good after a time. Once he gets three parts drunk his pain is gone, he don't feel nothing then. Could go to hell then. As soon as that's over, you're worse again. And Jesus, Mary and Joseph, he don't eat, he won't eat nothing. If he's in there three weeks in the hospital, all he'll have now, dinner time he'll have a drop of soup, nothing else.

He knows. He knows he's no better for it sure. But I remark on his drinking and he says to me, "What odds, old man? It's no better for me, what odds?" But in the meantime, if he'd look after hisself, he could live perhaps another couple year. He won't. No, he won't. I don't think he's going to live much longer. He can't eh? You can't live when you don't eat. "Old man," he said, "I got nothing to live for. What I got to live for now? I can't get outdoors, I can't walk, I can't do nothing, I got nothing to live for anyway. Better with me to be dead then be here in misery." I suppose it is better to be dead than in misery, we knows that. But that's not the thing: you're here and you got to stop till your time comes.

I got no other complaints, smothering that's all. Jesus, I had some pain there this morning when I got up. I had a mind to go see the doctor, but I don't like it. I know if I goes in there he'll want to keep me in there. I don't want to be in there. You chokes up see, you got a job to breathe when it's damp weather. When it's dry now it's not so bad. But foggy weather, that's the killer. I'm not too bad now, but Jesus, this morning me chest was paining.

We live on our pension now. We're getting one hundred and eighty dollars and sixteen cents each, that's what we gets. Old Age that is. We gets a rise in another three months, they're going to drive it up to two hundred dollars. We're well away now indeed. Yes, we got nothing to worry about now. No Compensation yet— I'm still hammering at it. The hang up on me is I worked away till I retired, that's what they got against me. But that got nothing to do with it. They're a bunch of . . . up there son. I suppose I'll get it after a time if I keeps at it.

It don't make much difference now anyway. We're here together and we're a happy couple, contented and that. Good enough with that. We're not young anymore. We don't go to no Times, or anything like that. In the days I go round; night time I stops home.

It's the fishing I misses most. Fishing was a good life boy. I liked everything about fishing. I was dory fishing, I was Banking and I was on the Beam Trawlers, aboard a Halibuter, everything. The way I look at it, I never seen no hard times. I never made nothing of hard times, I made the times just what they were. Now there it is. If I had it I'd put up with it, and if I didn't have it I'd put up with it just the same. That's the way it went along. Lots of times now we never had full plenty to eat, lots of times. I wasn't too often hungry, thank God for that.

Old Doctor Hollywood asked me one day was I nervous. I don't know if he thought I was nervous or what. "No, Jesus, boy I'm not nervous, I don't give a goddamn if I dies now." And I said, "I'm going to tell you something Hollywood son." "Yes," he said, "what is it?" I said, "When my time comes to die, brother, you or nobody else is not going to save me." He said, "You're right." I knows I'm right. I said, "The way I got it figured up, when I comes into this world I got to wait for me time to come. When that time comes I'm going to go out, nobody's going to stop me from going then." "Yes," he said, "that's about right."

Poor old Jack Byrne now, Alonzo Byrne and old Jock Andrews, they never lived no time. Because when they knowed they had it, they dwelled on it and that was it. Lost their nerve. All Jack Byrne does was walk the house all day long and all night long, cry and bawl the same as a youngster. Wouldn't eat nothing. When they knows they had it, they lost their nerve. They got down, see, thinking about it all the time. Once your nerve goes, that's it, you've had it. That's one thing thanks be to God I got, I got lots of nerve. I don't worry about nothing. You're dying, you knows you're dying, you got to put up with it.[1]

[1] Mr. Sullivan died in October of 1976.

4

You're not supposed to worry

ALPHONSE REILLY: At 44, all you see of 'Phonse are his gigantic eyes, his face's struggle not to reveal his hurt, and his weakened body.

He was a good father, a fine man. To start off with, he was about my age before he started to drink. He had a brother who was always drunk, and I suppose he was so poisoned bringing him home, he just didn't drink. He was always helping somebody, doing something for somebody. He did more for everybody else than he did home. He was into everything eh, into the co-op store here, and the union, and the football, everything like that.

Father didn't hit you that much unless you really did something bad. You'd have to steal something or break in somewhere, which wasn't very often then. We used to do a lot of devilment, but nothing to hurt anybody. Like you'd get in to steal a carrot out of a garden, and you'd go lie down and eat it. Well that was just the same as you rob a bank today. Oh yes, it was as big an offence to steal a carrot out of a man's garden as to rob twenty-five thousand dollars today. Probably punished for two weeks if you were caught. This is all we had eh, we had to get tensions off somehow. You'd probably get out in the old boy's garden, and make a noise so he'd know you were there so you'd get him to chase you. He'd probably chase you then out to that hill there; well he'd be pretty sick if he didn't catch you. And that was it. Father'd belt you then, then send you up to bed for the rest of the night for sure. And then stay in every evening after school, probably for a week.

I used to get more than anybody else because I was always at that, a real devil. You used to tie a handkerchief and lay it on the road with a piece of line; some old lady'd come along and pick it up, and you'd pull it out of her pocket. This sort of stuff. And you'd get a milk can like that and lay it down on the middle of the road with a piece of wire on it. A fellow'd come along kicking and you'd haul it away just before he'd go to kick it. Well he'd probably chase you right across the road. They prized cattle and sheep: you'd get a sheep and tie a can full of rocks round her tail. Every time it'd hit the ground, she'd go right through the air. She'd think somebody's throwing rocks at her.

The *biggest* crime then was you'd go into the shop, two guys working together, you're over talking to the guy and the other fellow'd be snitching candy. And then run out of there. I don't know if it was tension or not, but it used to come to you and you'd do it. Like I say, it was the only bit of enjoyment you'd have. You'd feel a little bit better after you'd do it. So I imagine it was the tension you were trying to get rid of.

We had to enjoy what we had the best way we could. Of course the school was something else again. We were always frozen. Jesus we froze to death. There was no glass broken then I'll tell you. All that woods over round the school, we cut all that to keep warm in the winter. You know those pot belly stoves; one of them up in this corner, well you're frozen down here. Only the guy was lucky enough to sit up close to the stove got his feet warm. The Grade Elevens had the preference anyway, there was only three of them in school at the time. I used to be glad to get out when my turn come to get the boughs. You'd get warm running around. You'd go out and break them off—it was right cold so they'd snap easy. Big armful, you'd come down and put them in the stove. You'd turn right red then. And the smoke, by Jesus the smoke, we used to do it for devilment, create a diversion. All hands would get up on the desks and walk around a bit see. We took all the stuff off the walls in the bathroom one year, this thick hairy stuff like Donnaconna. We took all that off, we had to to keep warm. We burned it. On those big old frosty days we used to stay home, it was too hard out to go to school.

The teacher would say, "All right, it's your turn to light the fire tomorrow morning," and you had to be in there at eight o'clock, get it warmed up for nine o'clock. So that evening then you'd go around and you'd pick up splits. You'd warm them in the oven all night till it was good and dry so it'd start off in the morning. You'd carry it up to school in the morning in a potato sack or something to keep the snow off. You'd have to go to the convent to get the key first thing, banks of snow up to the roof. You'd get the fire in. Three or four fellows used to work together. You'd have it going good when everybody got in. Then with the door opening and closing, the heat would be driven out. If you ran out of stuff then, that was it; whatever wasn't nailed down, that's was tossed in the stove. That was my best memories. I used to enjoy that.

The old man used to lace me, that was pretty often. Usually every day. Usually every day. Oh yeah, he used to pound me all the time. And if I didn't do something, the other kids would make up something, tell him I did this, tell him I did that. They weren't lying, I was always doing something. It began in earnest then, petty thievery. I suppose it was getting back at everybody. Then the lacings really came. I used to get it every day, for dessert. I got so used to it I was expecting it every day. I used to sit by the table, I got so used to it I used to sit down and wait for it to come, he'd only come look for me anyway. I got some tan. And the more he beat me, the more I did.

That's the way it kept up until I went to work in the Brook. I was nineteen. But not as much then because I was bigger. He couldn't hurt me anymore. I got to learn to roll with the blows. But I still never hated nobody. I don't know why he was always picking on me. I often felt like I hated the old man, but I didn't really. I still think he was a fine man. But I don't regret a thing today you know, except for the beatings of course, but I've forgotten them since that. He never cut me nor marked me. I resented more having to go to bed the rest of the night than the couple of clouts you got. The rest of them up listening to the radio, there used to be a lot of good shows on the radio—murder stories and all that and fights, and I couldn't get to listen to any of this because

I was in bed, punished. Same way in the morning. We used to have a lot of hens. The two older fellows, they'd have two eggs and I was only allowed one. Two slices of toast and they'd have three. They always had to have more than I did. I don't know why. I never figured it out. I give up trying.

I was always darting here trying to please everybody. I seen something to be done, I went and did it, hoping for a little pat on the head. The rewards were small I'll tell you. I often wished I was different. If the old man was really mad, he'd really drive you.

I did the same with him, the oldest boy, as the old man did with me. That's what got him where he's to today. I don't know why, but every time he blinked his eye, I'd draw off and belt him, for no apparent reason. He didn't do so good in his grades in school either, same as I did. And that would make me mad, so I used to belt him. He didn't empty the garbage for instance, that was reason enough for a big tanning. I could have done it quite easy myself and let him go on and have a bit of fun. So he ended up resenting that, and got in trouble two or three times. He wasn't like I was, because I never had nothing. You'd give him fifty cents, he'd go and break into something, with money in his pocket. So he ended up in Whitburn School for Boys, and he ended up in Mental Hospital—they figured there was something matter with him. He left that, headed up to Toronto, got into trouble up there and he got shoved in. He was there nine months. I must say he got straightened up. But he can't find nothing to do see. Can't get nothing for him. The Welfare won't give him nothing. What he's living on right now is what the Welfare is giving the rest of us. Now that's hard for a boy his age, especially today when everybody has pocket money, dances and everything like that. It's surprising he hasn't done something since he come home. He wants to be like everybody else. I must say he's taking it very good.

I never did have much of a brain. Like maths for instance. I used to love geometry, loved it. But I never could understand it. He explained it and it was as simple as two and two, but you get up to do the problem yourself and you just couldn't do it. When it was down on the board it looked so easy. But I never could do it alone.

I had to go to Burin Hospital to get my tonsils out one year and I developed pneumonia after that. I was out five or six months recuperating. Then I got used to the idea of being home, pampered a little bit. I never was before. So I didn't go back anymore. A fellow who used to teach drafting down at the Vocational School, he wanted me to go down at night time. I explained to him how hard it was. "No problem," he said, "I'm trained for that. No problem at all to make you understand." I never did go down. I should have went, I suppose. After that I suppose I would have had a good job somewhere, if I could have understood that. But we were up to so much devilment and that, we didn't used to study much at all.

I started mining in 1952. I was only down there eighteen months when I had to go to the San, the Sanitorium. The letter I got from St. John's was to go in for observation. They observed me for eight months before they sent me home. I was only supposed to do light work then. I used to bleed eh, I used to have periodic haemorrhages. I just could be sitting down like this, talking to you or anybody, and be a stick of blood on the window there. When it started to come up there was no way of holding it back, you could swallow all you like. Didn't have to cough, it just come. You'd open your mouth, and like a kid's water squirter.

When I left, Dr. Tuft was here at the time. He said, "You're not supposed to worry when you go up to the Sanitorium. You're supposed to get your drugs and do what you're told. No worries at all, only relaxation." Well, I left my wife here with what money I had when I went, I gave it to her. So she had to eat, eh? There was no more money coming in. The Welfare wasn't giving her anything. Dr. Tuft told me not to worry, he was going to straighten everything out with the Welfare Office. And all this was playing on my mind.

I was in there eight months. I don't know what way they do it now: every two months the Doctor would call you up and review your case, like a fella trying to get out on parole. Every two months, you'd get a notation in the night time that you were called up for a certain hour in the morning. Next morning you'd go up and he'd tell you if there was any difference, any change, if you were allowed out of bed or in bed, or what have you. Whatever he said, you had to do that for the next two months. So I did that for eight months.

I got married in January, '53, that was the same year I went into the San. I got married in January and I ended up in the San in September. I had a baby born in November and I didn't see it till the next June. She was six months old before I saw her, so you can imagine how I felt when I was in there. They tell you you're supposed to be happy while you're there. "If you got any problems bring them to us and we'll try to cure them up" and all this. And when the baby was born I got the telegram from Grand Bank. The wife was living in Lord's Cove with her mother. I had to pay for the telegram, plus the one that I sent back, "Congratulations, glad it's all over!" So they had me tortured about three weeks about that, till I got mad and told them where to go. Jesus, I was in there six months, and I didn't have any money. The old man, he'd send me a dollar or two, a couple packs of cigarettes.

So I got home in June, and Winnie was six months old—first time I laid eyes on her. You see the wife was on Welfare and she couldn't afford to come in and see me. Like if she was sick or something and the Doctor sent her in, then she could come in. She's a girl, completely deaf. She was here two months alone, in one end of my grandmother's house. I left her alone, six months pregnant. She stood it so long, and then I suppose she wrote to her mother, and the mother told her to come on out with her. Actually, what she got, her mother got for her from the Welfare Office in Grand Bank. Whoever this bastard was here wouldn't give her a thing.

Then I come home. She lived in Lord's Cove and I lived down here. Her mother and father wasn't too well off, there wasn't that much room up there, so I lived with my mother and she lived with hers. We used to see one another every other weekend, whenever I'd get a chance to go out. An odd weekend she'd come down. That's the way we lived for two years, three years. That was a hard go. It wasn't so bad for me because I was here with my own family, you know, brothers and sisters. But she was up there with nobody, her father and mother they were old. It was harder for her than it was for me really. I could go down with the boys and have a beer, shoot pool, something like that. She was always stuck around. We got our own house in '55. My first cousin owned this place, and he went to Toronto and he sold it to me for four hundred dollars. I got the priest to buy it, and I paid it back that way. That's how we come to live this place. So we been together ever since.

I was only supposed to do very light work, but there's no light work here. You either go in the mine or go fishing, and I didn't have nothing to go fishing with. There was no Incentives Programmes or nothing like that. You couldn't get a boat 'less you had the money to buy it. '56 I went to work in the school, janitor. All this time I was having haemorrhages. From nine to eleven to thirteen months I'd have a real big one, four and five days. I'd be in a private room four and five days, nothing to eat, just sucking ice cubes. I don't think they knows theirselves where the blood came from. In '65 the haemorrhages got real bad and I had to give it up altogether. I went on Welfare then. Dr. Hollywood gave me a paper that I couldn't work. I went on Welfare and I been on it ever since. I never got Compensation until July 16th last year. I only got $4300, that's all I got.

They classed me as 30% disabled, from the mine. I wrote to them after: different fellows classed 30% and was allowed to go to work and I was classed 30% and not allowed to go to work. They were getting more money than I was, and I had more kids too. Well, they came back and said I was classed as 30% from the mine, and not any other thing. So right now I'm not allowed to do nothing, not a thing. Supposed to take my time walking upstairs— actually, I'm not allowed to go up stairs at all if I can help it. If I had a bathroom down here I could stay down.

They classed me as 30% disabled; and right now I'm not allowed to walk upstairs, although I'm allowed to go out and make 70%. It don't make sense to me. And there's other fellows here, they're 30% disabled and they can work in Salt Cove Brook part-time. They got the same amount of money as I did, and still they're working in Salt Cove Brook and making a couple hundred bucks a week besides. I was on Welfare when I got this Compensation. We were getting something like $321 a month total. I got Compensation, and then there was a hundred something taken off that $321. Then we gets a letter from the Compensation Board that I was eligible for Special Fund. They sent me papers to sign and all that, number of kids, dependents. I filled all that out and got the Justice of the Peace to sign it—he charged me two bucks for signing all that. So I sent all that in, and I got $1300 Special Fund, that's for the kids now. So then the Welfare comes back and they takes out another hundred dollars for this. So actually I'm right back where I started afore I got Compensation. I gets $113 every two weeks from Welfare and a hundred dollars and thirty-three cents from Compensation. I was getting that in 1953 when I left Salt Cove Brook. Seven kids we got going to school. Hard to live boy, I'll tell you.

Right now most of my days are lying down. I got, there's a lot of names to them I can't say, but I got Bronchiactasis. I carry these around, every time I get a pain I put them under my tongue— nitroglycerine. If you're walking and you get a pain, stick one under your tongue and sit down wherever you're to. Supposed to bring you around after a while. It usually do. Very seldom you'll have to take two.

I don't sleep much, I don't get any sleep at all really. The last two nights now I went to bed at seven o'clock in the morning. I gets up around 10:30. I watch the news on television or the radio, I always listen to the late news. If there's a good show then I'll watch that; if not, I'll go to bed and read. I'll read till I gets tired, then I'll turn off the light and try to go to sleep. If I don't, I'll come down and watch TV some more, listen to the radio, do crossword puzzles.

The first thing I do mornings is turn on the radio and have a cigarette. Then I'll go up and see my mother if she's home. Wash the dishes with the wife. Take the dog for a walk. At fishing time I'll go and watch the fish come in. If I got a dollar or so in my pocket, I'll go down and shoot a game of pool. Most of the time I'm just content to lie back and watch TV. Lots of time I feel real bad most of the time. This last week for instance, it's just the same as somebody hit me with a stick from that end of town right around to the other side, every bone and muscle sore. I'm not used to sleeping built up in bed. You know, the doctor warned me, the danger of choking to death. I need at least four five pillows just sitting up in bed, and I'm not used to it—that's probably why I don't sleep that much. The bed is flat, eh, and all of a sudden you've got a forty-five angle, and your neck is broke when you do wake up in the morning. But I got a big pillow now, and then a smaller one and a smaller one and a smaller one, so there's a sort of curvature on it. It's a little better I think. The wife sews a bit on the sewing machine and she's after making different sizes for me.

I got hardening arteries really, that's one of the worst ones. Bronchiactasis, that's acute Bronchitis. Kidney trouble. My liver is down so far. I got a calcified lesion on the left lung, whatever that is. And a few other things I got. I don't have the dust though, that was before my time. Dust was when they used to drill holes with dry drills. They had water after I went in there. I suppose the Bronchiactasis came from this radon gas.

I was just sitting to the table reading the newspaper this morning. I started to cough, I had a cigarette in my hand. It was one of those long drawn out things where you can't get your breath back. I remember somebody coming in the door and that's the last thing I remember. When I came to, the wife was pulling me out from under the table. My head dropped on my hand with the cigarette, burned my eye. I broke the leg off the table there. I believe I was trying to get down on the floor. I remember falling on the floor the last time, but I didn't have time to get down there. No feeling at all. You're here and then all of a sudden you're not here. Like you die all together. It happened to my brother too, same thing. He started to cough: he made for the corner, like a cat falling down the side of a house, fingers stuck into the corner. It only lasts about three or four seconds. If it lasts any longer than that, you die. Your throat blocks off.

When I go to sleep, I don't cough. As soon as I opens an eye in the morning, that's it, it starts again. I'm resigned to the fact. Dr. Hollywood told me that I got practically the same as my father had —he died of a heart attack. And I got all the same symptoms, the same feelings, according to what he used to tell me. So I'm just waiting for the inevitable. I don't know when, could be twenty years, could be next week. So there's nothing I could do. For instance, if there was a paling off the fence and I went out to put it on, well I'd probably have to sit down and take one of those pills under my tongue. So no point in planning to stick up a fence or build a storm door, nothing like that. The only thing I can look forward to is walking down the street to see if there's any fish coming in. Hard thing to say for a forty-four-year-old man, isn't it? Eh? Well that's all I can look forward to.

Of course they improves on everything every day, the drugs and what have you. I haven't got a breathing problem now like I used to have: the breathing got so bad I couldn't see. I was on the ward at the hospital at the time, it was two o'clock in the morning. I had gone in that evening, and I wasn't too bad. He told me if I felt it coming on to go in. When I sat on the toilet, it was like everything was coming in; the walls, the ceiling, the floor coming up. I ended up on the children's ward, under one of the kid's beds, with all my pyjamas tore off trying to get some air. But my breathing isn't too bad since that, so long as I don't walk too fast.

I lost two uncles and my father, two brothers-in-law. And there's a good many fellows to go yet. I worked with one fellow, he was only thirty-two when he died. My wife's brother, he was thirty-six. One hundred and fifty-four, I think, the last time I counted them—and there's a lot of fellows after going since that. When my father was alive we sat down one night; we were naming them off and he was marking them down. That's what we came up with, 154. There's a lot of fellows my age to go yet, they're still working in there. It's surprising they're there that long. Course a lot of them are hardened to it. They're getting used to it.

Fellows got to be thinking about it. The fellows that did think about it, they're gone. Great big fellows. Christ, they're only young but they're about 215, 230 pounds, just went down to 112, 98 pounds. One fellow next door, Jack Byrne, he literally went up the wall. The Doctor told his sister and brother that he'd go crazy, he was that nervous over himself.

I've seen fellows sit down, friends of mine, and we'd played cards with them, drank together, had house parties. They'd sit down like you and I are, and cry like a baby and say, "Just imagine, this time next year I won't be here." Almost make you cry yourself. I seen them do that, three or four of them. They were right.

The wife's brother there, Frank, the fellow we was talking about. March 3rd he went into the hospital first, with a pain in his back. September 9 he died, with a hole in his back as big as your fist. Wouldn't heal up, that's where it came out, right over his ribs on his spine. His wife had a baby two weeks before he died. His wife, she went around screeching, saying, "Thank God, the baby's only two weeks old, and the father just died!" It didn't take him long, from March to September.

Real tough fellows, they're determined "I'm going to get well." One fellow in particular, Joe Parsons his name was. Some fellows'd say, "He's not looking very well." "Ah, that's nothing son, I'm going to get better too"—I can see him right now; his two eyes are like two holes burnt in a blanket, sunken right back, his old cheekbones sticking out here, almost like a skeleton. But he was real determined. He'd hang on and hang on month after month. There were other fellows, they'd be dead in a month, gave up and cry, this sort of thing. Big fellow over here next door, he cried himself to death in a matter of a couple of months. Everytime he'd look out the window, he'd see something, he'd remember it, and he'd say he weren't going to see this no more. He was an easy-going man, a good father, hard working.

But there's not a man left around here, all this area. About six houses that way, and as far as the Town Hall that way. Not a man left. Except this fellow that lives next door here; he never worked in the mine.

My father, he knew it. He knew it a couple of years before he got after it. He knew there was something wrong, but he didn't know what it was, or how to go about exposing it until Jack Windish and Dr. de Villiers come here. He wanted to take a sample of air in her kitchen, and that was over the safe level in her kitchen. It was actually over the safe level. Most of them blames Joey Smallwood. I suppose that was an election gimmick too. They came here that time, and the people of St. Lawrence was supposed to get a million dollars a year. A million dollars a year, half from the Company and half from the Government. That was seven or eight years ago, and we haven't got a million dollars here yet, not all together. A million dollars is a lot of money. There's 150 of us here: you multiply 150 by two hundred dollars a month. That's no million dollars.

I used to wire a lot of houses. I was a pretty good electrician, did a lot of commercial wiring, houses and stores and what have you. That used to take up most of my time. Then the Welfare got mad, and everybody phoning in and writing letters. I didn't mind that. After all, most people are keeping me anyway you might say, by paying taxes. Whatever money I used to make, I used to mark it down. Whatever was over, I'd pay it back. So after a while I got so sick I couldn't do it anymore.

In 1968 I took a course in watchmaking, a correspondence course, and I'm at that ever since. That little cabinet down there, that's watch parts. I was at it four or five years before I decided to take a course in it. I got fascinated by it. Little woman's watches, I used to take it all apart and put it back together again. So I took the course in it. It cost me eight hundred dollars. I took it in the States, from the Chicago School of Watchmaking. They sent me two different watches: they'd break it and send it to me to repair it, and when you'd send it back to them they'd grade it. There was a lot of tools went along with that, little screwdrivers. The only help I got from the Rehabilitation when I came out of the San was the names and addresses of where to buy parts.

I fixed a few radios. As a matter of fact, I don't turn away anything. They comes to the door and I takes it in. It got to be in pretty bad shape if I don't repair it. Probably make a very good living if you had a store, with a warehouse or something in back to store your parts in. An appliance repair store, that's what I had in mind. But I never had any capital to start anything. When the Small Loan thing came out, I was afraid to go ask anybody there, afraid they wouldn't give it to me. Figured I was a risk on account of being sick; you know, I wouldn't be able to pay it back, might drop dead before it was half paid back.

When I was in the San there was nine of us in there from here. There was a little fellow there, he was only nine years old then. He's married now up in Labrador. We're the only two left, out of nine. I was one of the fortunate ones I guess.

5

I sold me boat
this morning

*SAMMY BYRNE: At 46, his speech punctuated by an
explosive laughter that sounds like weeping, his mirth-
less eyes dispassionately record the waves of anxiety
spasms which rack his body.*

I sold me boat this morning, the first time I was without a boat
since 1939. I sold it this morning. That was the hardest thing I
done in me life. But I had to. I can't use her, eh? It was one of
those grey swamps. I sold me boat this morning, and all me gear. I
couldn't use it, and if I couldn't use it it's no good to me. I fished
twenty-six years, all me life, on top of working.

I was rotten yesterday, and I was rotten the day before. If I does
any little thing—I went down hauling in me boat and baling the
water out of her—well I never got the better of that for half the
night. If I just sits down here or goes for a drive, that's fine. But if
I do too much stooping or walk up the hill too fast . . . and I forgets
about it, eh, cause it's not that easy to knock off working after
thirty years. I've got that shifted before I realizes I shouldn't touch
that.

The worst part of it is to sit down here and watch everybody else
going to work, that's what I'd say is the hardest part of this. I'm
going to work ever since I was nine years old eh? Now you just
have to sit down and watch the guys going to work. I started in the
mine when I was only fourteen year old. Here then you had to
start if you wanted to live. I went aboard a boat when I was nine

year old. I sold me first quintal of fish in 1939 for three dollars and thirty-seven cents; nine years old. I was one of ten, and if I wanted to eat I had to work. It took all hands for to keep ten youngsters without you were going to Welfare, and that's something I never had much use for.

There used to be four Byrne brothers in the mine. Tommy's sick with Silicosis longer than I am, Isaac is sick, but it's not Silicosis I don't think he got, don't know what it is, he's got a lump coming in his groin. But it's something the same eh, because it don't have to be the lungs. It's after affecting a lot of people in the throat, everywhere. The rest of them wasn't down that long.

People think a mine is just a hole. But it's not, it's a small world down there. After you gets down there five or six years it gets in your blood. A miner is a miner. And there's always something different so there's challenge to it. You're drilling bad ground and you figures you can drill it or you can't drill it. You makes a lot of decisions.

They were tough. They were contrary, to be truthful about it. The only thing they liked more than a fight was two fights. I wouldn't want to see a German or a Newfoundlander look down at those fellows and tell them something they didn't like. A foreman, he said something the fellow didn't like and the fellow picked him up like that. The other fellow said "lay him down," so he laid him down on the bank. The other fellow said, "I didn't mean there, I meant down that hole," that's two hundred feet below. Boy they were awful when I went there first. You had to just watch and say nothing. But I wasn't long before I was just as bad as any of them.

A foreman's no good down there. Every miner is a foreman. He knows what he got to do down there. What can a foreman do down there only give orders through his wicket? But if he's not going to do his job down there when you gives him what you wants him to do through your wicket, you needn't go down and try to make him do it because he's got every way of bluffing you. You've just got to depend on their own skill and their own will. There's no miner goes down there wants to sit down; he don't want nobody to drive him either. He knows what he got to do. When he goes down there to do a certain job, he's going to do it, any possible way he's going to do it. I know I had to stay back so

57

high as a half hour to get one drift round. I drilled twenty-six holes in that and I wanted the other two, and if they kept the compressors going I was going to have those two and fire the round. Not for the sake of what I was getting for it. If I says two rounds today, I want two drift rounds; no one's forcing me to do that, but whatever I had in me mind. And if I drill that today and she comes good, I try to drill it better tomorrow. And if I could use less powder today, I'd try to use less again tomorrow.

Management never understood that. They figured everybody there was trying to do them. Mine Captain knew when he was sending men down there in the smoke, he knew he was doing wrong. But what choice did he have? If he didn't do it, somebody else would. But now there was more behind them eh, there was bigger shots behind them pushing them on. He knew so well as I did, for I was down there when as high as seven was gassed in two hours, just dropped down. That was everywhere then cause we had no air. Your orders was to leave on the compressor for one hour, blow smoke for one hour, then shut off the compressors. Maybe they didn't want to wear out the compressors blowing air.

Them miners, you can't get them nowhere else in the world like you can in St. Lawrence. It's just a laugh to say that they can. They'll bring in a bunch of miners today and next week they got no one. I seen miners coming here from other mines. They stayed long enough to see what that place was like and got out fast. They never seen no ground shifting around like that; you see seven or eight hundred tons shifting around alongside of you. You're drilling a round now, you goes to lunch and when you comes back that round was out and probably a thousand ton along with it. There's the kind of nerve and guts you got to have to work that place.

It'd make you sick to your stomach. We got fifteen-year miners, twenty-year miners in there. One of them miners, he figures he wants to shift off and stay home; tomorrow morning he'll get a warning slip. One of the lead miners! From someone down there don't know one end of that mine from the other. I seen them stay home a couple hours for a football game—they'll get a warning. Twas only a week ahead of that they were down trying to dig out bodies, perhaps for thirty-five, forty hours. I'll put it like one of me buddies put it one time we were on a grievance with Siebert and the Corporation: he said, "Look, if we can handle the local slime, we can handle the rest of ye."

The worst were this Silicosis, when it got far enough ahead where you could see there was something killing the miners. The miners don't pay much heed to bad ground or somebody being killed—that's another accident, happens everywhere. If someone got killed you thought hard of it, but that was it, it was an accident. We were watching out for bad ground and trying to avoid what accidents we could, when the things was there was killing us we couldn't see!

Most of the times you gets a warning. A lead miner, an experienced miner, he knows when to leave that ground. We used to say when the ground starts to talk to you, what it's saying is it's time to get out. Now the different air blasts is a different kind of sound; there's some that you can stay there with and there's more you can't. Some air blasts you'll get just like that, more she'll blast a dozen times before she come.

A lead miner, he got a good idea of what's going on. He'll make lots of good decisions too although he don't get the feather for it. There's some joker they'll bring over here from Germany, somewhere like that, and they'll tell you what to do. There's always those fellows that they're bringing over here. They're going to tell he, fellows in there twenty years a miner, how to do it down there even though he doing it twenty-five years and doing it safe. Mine Captains; you can get them anywhere for a dollar a dozen, and I told them. If the truth hurts them that's just too bad. I spent too many hours down there.

I was lowered under water, me and another fellow. When the hoistman was given the bell to take us up, he shoved the wrong control and we went down, skip (mine elevator) and all, under eight feet of water. I didn't mind that. I opened the hatch that was in the roof. This fellow that was with me, he's dead now, I don't know what he had in his mind, there was only one thing in his mind right then and that was to hold on. I had a job to get him clear. He was the Mine Captain too. I said to him, "What happened to you?" And he said, "The only thing what come to me was to hold on when that cold water struck me." A poor place to hold on, down there eight feet. We had the pumps off then for five or six hours, something went wrong with the power. But you just jumped out into that, swum around, got your gear. You never got half gear enough, you only run the mine the best way you could. We put the pumps back on before we come up; just another dipping to us. If you had stopped to dry yourself off, probably thirty, forty men'd have to come off night shift. You had to keep them pumps going. I had nineteen pumps going on nine different levels, and you have to know what you were doing to keep that place dry.

It wasn't an affiliated union then in the Forties, just more or less a group of men. We got certified with the A. F. of L. first, and then we had to break away from that; they were doing us more hurt than good. That's the same bunch that Joey drove out.

In the beginning you just done what you were told if you wanted to stay there. They had one word before the union got strong enough, they'd still use that now if they could—"you do that or go home"—when they gives you something. If they sent some fellow home, all hands come home when they got far enough ahead to get that group together. I know one time a couple of the miners got into the cab of the truck driving home, and just because he didn't get out for to let the foreman get in, they wanted to give him a shift off. Now that man was going underground for eight hours; that foreman could sit down by the stove and dry hisself for eight hours if he wanted to.

The Assistant Manager that was in there the strike before last, he just spoke a little bit in favour of the crew were on strike. He said it in the Staff Club, all the staff was there. And he was half drunk when he said it. "What the strikers are looking for here," he said, "they should have got a year ago." The next morning I seen the letter, he showed it to me: "Your service is no longer required." "Now," he said, "I don't want *their* services if that's the kind of bunch they got working." He's that kind of fellow: he was a good man to work for, he wanted to see the men get fair play too. He belonged up there in Manitoba. "I'm not missing much, am I," he said, "they can't hurt me."

That's how childish some of them people are. We got a strike, not the last strike we had, the one before. We were off six months. We could have ended that in one day. And they wouldn't take a chance on going over there and talking to the union men. Any one of them, we didn't care who it was—the Manager, Assistant Manager, the Labour Officer—we invited he over to hear our side of it to carry it back. We wanted to talk. We could have ended it right there, I knew it meself. We didn't want no more money; we wanted the same money package, but we wanted across the board for every man to get the same. The Company had nothing to lose, just take the money that was there. They were going to give us $100,000 anyway, so why not spread it? That's the way we wanted it. But that strike went on for five months after that, and they had to give us the same thing in the end.

It was all battles. You were fighting a losing battle all the time because the people couldn't say ought. There was only one way you can beat any of them companies, with time. It was like the second last strike we had with Alcan; we had them beat but they also had most of the people. A lot of them wasn't like me. I had a fishing rig, I could make a living any day. I didn't go into Alcan last time cause I had to go to make a living, I had to go because I had nobody to fish with me. The mining here put out everything else; we got a mine and that's it. Every young fellow here now is a miner. And they're still one of the lowest paid around: I don't mean every miner, there are a few fellows on contract got a thousand dollars this week. You don't hear nothing about the fellows coming down with eighty-five and ninety. One of the biggest companies in Canada is Alcan and they're paying less than four dollars an hour.

The Union wasn't that good in the Forties, but it was still something. You could have a five month strike and end up with a ten cent *cut*. That's right, that really happened in the Forties. People just had to go back. The Union President, when he signed them papers, he figured he was getting a ten cent rise, but somehow they wiggled that around when we got it we were getting ten cents less than what we were getting before. They were back then; any of those deals you're back to work before you gets anything about it; it's usually on a paper what they're going to give you. And some of them fellows is so clever, they can put something on paper and when it comes to work out, it's not the same at all. To somebody like me it'd look good, but you take it now and it's going to look a whole lot different when you explains it.

The Company and the Government don't want to hear tell of the Union anytime. But in the States, they had leaders could come

61

and explain to the people and get it through to them. See, our Union Presidents down through the years was just another miner. You take Herb Sullivan, he's got his Grade Eleven, but he's just another miner. He's still working for the Company for that matter. I say he's doing a good job for what he knows about it. It's a job for the best lawyer in Canada, to try to talk to them lawyers comes down here. Any of us, probably with Grade three or four, and you got Alcan's lawyers representing the Company to talk to you. You got to sit down with them. Now what can we do with a bunch like that? They can swindle that around to suit theirselves. Half the time you wouldn't know what they were talking about. They mixes it up with the percentage of this and that, holiday money all mixed up in the one deal; well they had it right big. But when you got it figured out, you never had nothing. That's the last thing you know, how much money they're giving you. They figures the miners is ignorant, eh?

The Union gets pretty hot here in St. Lawrence. Even the women was out here picketing that pier. One of the crowd belonging to the Company set it off one night; he bumped a woman with the car trying to get through. That was four years ago. They definitely weren't going to load that boat. The youngsters would have killed every man with rocks, they all swore that. And that was getting bad cause they were up there among the houses throwing rocks and you didn't know where they were coming from. That took six months; we did get sixty-five or seventy cents out of that. One of the guys in the Company said they'd starve them back, he couldn't care less if all hands starved.

They say they'll close down the mine. Now I can't see that, but if they got no more interest than that, I say they should be closed down and let somebody else work it. *There's* where they made the big mistake; the Government must of all been asleep to sell Alcan the Corporation. They just give it to them. They give them all the claims and everything else. They got ore tied up, none of it's mined out, and Alcan got all the claims. They might not want it for the next hundred years, they got more than they can handle right now.

You take those companies, eh? The St. Lawrence Corporation worked there for over thirty years and they left nothing for the town. And some joker'll come in and say, "Look at the Recreation

Centre what Alcan gave the town of St. Lawrence." Every youngster in St. Lawrence don't care if that place burns down in there. All of them was expecting ice in that Recreation Centre: when they never got ice, they couldn't care if they never got anything. There's two great big graveyards over there to pay for that. I worked with 180 men on that job, and there's 142 of them in the graveyard.

St. Lawrence I would say would have another 150 homes. But who was going to resettle in a gas chamber? So far as I'm concerned meself, Hitler's gas chamber was a King alongside of that place. Cause he only took two minutes to do away with thousands; and a man got to come home from that job and spend five or six years dying, melting off the face of the earth. I mean somebody that don't know those people don't know what they goes through. You go three or four months and see somebody next door, and every day you go he's a bit smaller, and by and by there's nothing left, only the bones. He can't even talk to you, he can't talk to nobody belonging to him. Dr. Hollywood'll keep him alive for six months longer than any other doctor in the world can, because he knows what he's doing. He's doing it, he's doing it this last ten year. And I know he wonders hisself is he doing right, lots of times. But like he said, that's his job.

The ministers and the priest, they never helped or hindered. They just stayed out of it. They had the very least to say as any of the rest of them. There's only one thing you can make out of it; they gets their wages, their living, and that's all they care. All they wants is a great big money plate, that's the way I got them sized up. I can't swallow all they thinks.

The Company *was* the Government at that time. I wouldn't say it's much better yet. It was more or less a Government racket. They were spending Government money, it was just Government loans keeping her going. Siebert wasn't spending his money. People worked for nothing to get this thing going, hours and hours for nothing. They had no trucks, so they hauled it on oxen and slides, horses and cows, anything that could haul a quarter of a ton of fluorspar. Our first Member, he come up here when all the people were dying, first coming up with Silicosis. He went to see a man was dying with it and they went to St. John's. The man still died with it, but he wrote it in the paper that it was Silicosis. There was so much pressure on him he had to go back and write an apology. He wrote an apology!

I come up and I was feeling miserable. I went fishing for a year and then I went back underground again. But I seen I couldn't do it. I had to walk up; I couldn't get up. I had to force meself. The last hundred feet I walked I was over an hour getting up. I had to, I had two boys going to school. I had me own home, I had to go to work. I don't care if I die in there, I'm not going to be hungry, I never growed that way. I went back before against doctor's orders, but I went back for the same reason—I knew I wasn't going to get nothing. I went down from roughly seven thousand dollars last year to seventy-five dollars a month Compensation, and that's all I'm getting yet, and thirty dollars from the Special Fund. She keeps herself see, only for the wife we would have starved to death on that.

The trouble with this "30%", eh? We got dozens of people here 30% disabled and they're going to work, same as I did. Some of these days they're going to have to bring them home same as they did me. I was feeling so miserable I wouldn't take no chance on driving the machine meself. I couldn't bring me tool box or nothing the last evening. I had to get another fellow to bring that. I told him, "You can bring that up and you can heave it to Hell."

Who wants to hire you if you're 30% disabled? How can you give a man a day's work with 30% of his lungs gone? Those Alcan doctors, they come every year, they give you the biggest kind of a medical. They take you apart almost; they wouldn't even give you a report. A lot of fellows they put on light duty. So I asked the Doctor, I caught him unawares I suppose, I asked him in his opinion what would light duty be. And he told me, "Like cleaning up fittings, painting something—I wouldn't recommend sweeping the floor, it's too dusty." I said, "Well I'll tell you the light duty I seen a couple fellows on yesterday. One of them was out digging a trench, the other fellow was out driving posts, the other fellow was up packing up cement up seven bags high. You call that light duty?" It was only a couple year ago they took a fellow out of the mine and put him on light duty: and he died packing up cement eight, ten bags high. He fell down, and they brought him home. A month afterwards he was dead. This is their light duty.

Now I don't see how some fellows say you can go into Salt Cove Brook and go on light duty. I spent a long time on that job and I don't see no light duty there. I don't see any place where if I was foreman I could give a man light duty. It's not there to give. You can't give somebody something that don't exist. Anything belonging to a mine, you needn't look for nothing under fifty pounds. Now there might be the odd job, eh? Like in the tool crib. But sure, everybody can't go in there. I know a buddy of mine went back in there on light duty—he wasn't getting enough to live on, so he went back to work—and for to give he a job in the light duty they had to take a man out of there was sick, was sixty-two-year-old, worked over thirty year with that job, and put he in.

The Company, they're getting a bit better. The Union'll straighten them out. Like a few years ago a fellow got killed: they were only going to give so much to his funeral, said they were going to pay up to $150 to get a fellow home if he got killed. A half quare fellow, a buddy of mine, said to them, "What are you going to do if you gets to a beaver pond and the $150 is gone? Going to bury him in the beaver pond?" You know, the small, rotten things they come up with.

Something that do hurt me now is when I see a young fellow with his Grade Eleven going in to Salt Cove Brook, going down into that gas chamber. Cause it's still a gas chamber. I don't care. I tell anyone—there's a lot of them don't like it. A lot of them ask me opinion on it. I know one time last year a young fellow come up to me, "I'm getting laid off," he said, "I'm going to ask you something. I wants you to make a decision for me." I says, "I'm not making no decision for nobody, son. I'll give you an opinion, but I don't make no decisions for nobody." "Well," he says, "if you were in my place, what would you do? I can be laid off, or I can go in the mine." "Well," I says, "son, I'll make that one for you. You go home; wash the dishes for your mother, but don't go underground. I had seventeen year underground and I wouldn't have seventeen seconds had I known what was down there. Right now, look, you can go where you like. I'm here, I'd have the devil to get up to the car. Now there it is." "That's good enough," he says, "I'll get out of there this evening." So he stayed home the winter and went back on the surface in the spring. Me own two fellows; one fellow works on the surface in there. The other guy, he won't even go over the hill. There's ne'er one of them going underground while I'm alive.

That's where I made me big mistake. I should have stayed fishing. There's a lot of times I would have had less money than I had when I was in the mine, but I'd also be able to work today which I can't now. Right now I got three pills dinner time, three breakfast time, three supper time; and I got a bottle in me pocket. If I goes to walk up that hill I got to take one of them. I don't take it till I gets the pain. And when I do get up there, I got to stop and get me breath before I can go anywhere else.

It's going to kill every man that's there today. You can't tell me any different from that. But where it took it fifteen year to get us, it's going to take it twenty-five to get them. It's that much better. But it's still there: only time's going to prove that out, but that's the way it's going to come out.

I went aboard the CN boat the other year. I sat down in the chair and I listened to two doctors talking about all the widows in St. Lawrence getting twenty, thirty thousand dollars from the Compensation. I heard them telling how the widows leaves St. Lawrence and goes into St. John's to pick up their grub, and how much money the widows got. I got boiled right up. Jesus, I wasn't long before I was going down his throat. I said, "Son, listen. I don't know who the two of ye are, I couldn't care less, but it's jokers like you who give the St. Lawrence miners so much trouble. I'm one of them fellows you're talking about. Look, I worked with them, I lived with them, I ate with them, and I slept with them. Them miners you're talking about now that their widows got $20,000: the widows in St. Lawrence lived for years on forty, forty-five dollars a month, and *some* of them, the value of their Compensation was $20,000. All that it took out of them when they were trying to get twelve or fourteen youngsters through school had to come out of that $20,000. It's a long drive from St. Lawrence to St. John's to get a box of groceries," around about seven hundred miles back then. "But it's jokers like you that's the crowd we're trying to fight. Fellows that talk but don't know what they're talking about." They just clammed right up, they froze.

Walter E. Siebert, he's the owner of the St. Lawrence Corporation. When he come here, he come here with the plan when he'd get money enough, he'd pull out. That's just what happened. His son told me that. He told me, "When the old man gets money enough out of this, he's going to pull out, and to hell with St. Lawrence." And that's just what he done.

There's whole families here wiped out. It's time for someone to make a noise.

6

Only one fellow
ever suffered more than I

HARRY ANDREWS: His immense body grotesquely swollen by mine disease and battered by a mine accident, he has endured a quarter of a century of almost continuous pain.

In the hard Thirties I was growing up, in Lorries. Me father belonged to here all right, but he went to Lorries as a young fellow, went fishing with one of them old Frenchmen what run away from France and come to Newfoundland. He fished with them all the time, and I suppose he started going out with me mother then. Her old man was pretty well off, he had traps of his own and he had a shop of his own. Well off he was. The old man married her and he lived up there till the Thirties. We come down here then.

We reared ourselves up. The old man was always away working somewhere. He used to work in St. Pierre on them rum runners, that was the only job you could get then. Me mother died years before that, I can't even remember her at all. No school. If we were going to school it was up to ourselves whether we went or no. If you felt like going to school, well you could go.

Lots of times I seen we never had a mouthful in the house. We went over to the merchant there and he wouldn't give us nothing. The old man and another fellow went up and said, "If we don't get it, we got to take it." They took the bag of flour. That's all they took, their flour. And he went to jail for that. Pretty hard if you was in the house and had four or five small youngsters; couldn't get nothing to eat and the merchant wouldn't give you nothing. You couldn't see them there crying for something to eat and you with nothing to give. If there was any way of getting it, you'd get it. I would, I know. Whatever way I could get it, I'd have it.

I was around ten. Buddy said, "Harry, there's something the matter with you." "No boy," I said, "there's nothing wrong with me." "There's something wrong," he said, "did you have anything to eat today?" "No, that's one thing I never had. Nothing to eat." He carted me over to the house and gave me something to eat. Pretty hungry that day. I was ten. Lots of times I had nothing to eat. Sure you wouldn't get nothing when you did get anything. You wouldn't get no milk or butter or nothing like that, we didn't know what any of that was when we were growing up. Or sugar. Just bread and molasses. You'd think yourself lucky if you had bread. And then if you had put molasses on your bread, you couldn't put any in your tea. Sure if you did there'd be only for a couple days, and for the rest you'd have nothing. I seen one fellow here perished; rotted he did in his bed. I went down there, and me son, he had nothing in the house, only a salt mackeral. That was the only thing in the house to eat.

You never used to stop then. When the spring of the year come you'd have to get ready and go fishing with your father. Before it was over, you had to cut the hay and make it if you had any hay or any ground. When that'd be over then you'd have to attack the woods, try to cut wood enough for the winter. Then you had to haul that home; you had ne'er horse, you had to haul it on a hand slide, to keep the stove going. And then every time kelp come in you had to be down there loading that up. It take so much of that, you'd bring up a pile as big as this house: two or three days after that, it'd be half as big, it used to rot away that much. It was great stuff to grow potatoes, that mossy kelp.

The young fellows here got nothing to do. Not like when we were growing up. As soon as we got big enough to see over the side of a dory, we were fishing with our fathers. Never stopped, winter and summer, the hardest kind of work. The young fellows are in school now till they're twenty year old, three parts of them. I'd live to be a hundred if I had the comfort this crew's got.

I started on Iron Springs in '39, and worked there a couple of years. Oh me son, shocking in regards to the smoke and everything like that. I went mucking first and then I went helping with poor old George Byrne. Times we couldn't see one another, with no water on the drill. The dust, me son, you'd have to haul it out of your nose. You'd be snow white with the dust.

I was married then, but I was married to a different woman. The woman's dead now; she wasn't well the whole time we were married. We claimed it was TB. I don't know if it was or not. Her brother died of the same stuff; she used to go down and do for him, shave and everything like that. That's what he died of, TB, and we figure she got the germ from him. No hospital or nothing then; you'd think with TB they'd put her in the San, wouldn't you? She was the same as I was here the other day because her legs was so big. She was only a small woman, her legs was as big as me waist before she died. After she died, I had the youngsters in the orphanage. They were in there a long time.

They got a lot more air now than what we had. We had no air at all. When we go down we couldn't see one another in the smoke. And the first few years starting off, when the other crew come up, we had to go straight down. And you'd be going down in all this smoke when they'd be just after blasting. Now they has four hours blowing smoke before the other crew goes down. So they got it better that way. I don't believe they're even allowed to drink the water down there now; the place we were drinking the water out of, boiling kettles for lunch time, that's the worst place for radiation there was in that drift.

We used to get gassed down there, conked out. We'd be right out, stone dead with no air in the world. Lots of times. There used to be lots of gas there, mucking up that dry muck. You'd have a rest for a little while, not too long, and then go start again. That all depends on the kind of foreman you had; some was the best kind, more wanted everything done.

Some pretty good foremen down there. We had some bad ones too. I had one fellow down there; I used to figure he had naught to do about me because I was on the pumps, that was me job, and he had his job—look after that. He'd crawl, trying to catch me sleeping in that pump house. He ne'er ever caught me though. He'd wait till he figured I was asleep. I'm not saying I didn't have a scattered nap in there, I had lots of them. I worked a week's work in there without coming up, working other fellow's shifts who was sick. I was better off then than I was home because I was home by meself. I'd sooner stay in than come home, nice and warm down there. You had the real comfort on the pumps, nice concrete house.

It wasn't too good in Salt Cove Brook then boy. Always power trouble. Water, me son. But down to Iron Springs, that's where the water was, coming down through the chutes like some kind of a river. You had to wear oil clothes so the water'd go down your back. It'd go down your neck, everywhere. I went into Salt Cove Brook then, working on the pumps. It was all right, there was no work to it. Talk about water; me son, you lose the power for ten minutes and it'd be up and down you. I was often there up to me arms in water, trying to save the pumps. And you'd be there at that all night long, froze to death.

I had the accident in '44. I got beat up in the mine in Salt Cove Brook. The roof come down on me, a big slab. Alec Tarrant was there with me, Joe Malone and Paddy Power, two of them dead now. They went up in the bucket and I was there scraping it up. The wall was smooth just like concrete, like you smoothed it off with a trowel. So by and by Joe Malone makes a screech at me to get out of the way. If I'd stayed where I was at, probably I wouldn't have got hurted—or perhaps I would have got killed. When he made a screech, I made a jump, and I jumped right under her. I could feel the shattering down over me, that's all I knows. I felt it first hitting the hat to smithereens. They were there and they couldn't get me out from under it. It was across me, one big slab. After a while they got me out and carried me out and laid me down. I didn't think I was hurted. They started calling the cage with the danger signal—if anything goes wrong, you ring nine bells —and she wasn't long in coming I'll tell you. And that's all I knows. I went out cold then and didn't know nothing else.

They tells me I was there a long time on that table, an old wooden table. An old doctor was here then, I don't know if he was even a doctor. And the blood was everywhere. The blood was over the tops of their shoes, so much was coming out of me. The shovel went into me side, they said, and I was busted open and me hip was all crushed up. Me leg was broke, I was all beat up down around me privates. Was there all night and all the next day. They couldn't get nothing to carry me to Burin, we had no hospital here then. The pain. I was unconscious most of the time. A little boat happened to be here from Point au Gaul; they were working on a house here and staying aboard her. Anyway, they got me to Burin and then they got me to St. John's from that. The priest come, fixing me up for the other world. He thought I was dying.

The Doctor here, he was only a horse doctor, that's all. Sure when I got beat up, he never done nothing with me in there. He had me on the table with the blood running out of me in gallons. He only just come in and peep in at me, wouldn't even give me a needle for it. He figured in a matter of minutes I'd be dead. But I wasn't. I was there till the old man come in. He was going to kill the Doctor. He give me the needle then. All he do then the whole way to St. John's was come peep through the door, wouldn't come no handier.

After I got to St. John's, the nurses there didn't think I was going to get better. The Doctor thought it too. The pelvis, that got bent in and never come out. I'm different on one side than the other see. That was all crushed up. Even after I got better, you rub your hand and it just like bones sticking out through the skin. Little bones. They're not there now.

I couldn't make no water. They had to put a tube into me stomach. I still couldn't do it when I come home. I still can't do it. I got to lie down. Whenever I wants to make me water, I got to lie down. They never cured me if I'm still like that, did they? I goes through more pain me son with that. I figures there's only one more fellow ever suffered more than I'm after suffering, and that's Jesus Christ. And that was only while He was carrying the cross and dying on it. But I'm at it this last thirty years. When I wants to make me water, I go in there and stand over that toilet. I could be there an hour before a drop came. When it do come, perhaps it'd be drop drop drop. And I have the worst kind of pain while that's going on. Same as you had a cramp in your stomach. Well that's the way I be all the time.

The way it is with me water, I can't make me water and I can't hold it. I'm right bursting to do that now. Say I were ready to do it and somebody in the bathroom, I'd be right busting to do it and wouldn't be able to hold it dropping out of me. Before I got married to her, I used to spoil more shorts like that; they'd get soaking wet and I'd take them off and heave them away and go get another pair. I'd be right busting to do it and it'd be right dropping out of me, dropping out of me. I'd get in and stand up over the tub. I'd be going mad with the pain, and still the same, just dropping. And then perhaps after a long time it'd start to dribble a bit. I wouldn't pass no more than half a glass full, that was all.

The legs are down now. But it won't be long. They're starting to swell now, look. When it does that, you presses in and the dent stays there. There's water in them now already. When I went into the hospital this time, I couldn't get nothing on me feet, only the socks. I don't know what's causing it. The leg was big, black and blue; she looked like she was going to bust when I went to hospital. Late last fall was the first time I noticed it. They tap them and drain them. I never asked them what it was. I don't ask them. They never tell you the truth anyway.

Oh yes, I'm working all the time ever since. I be working till '61, and the doctors never turned me down then. I couldn't walk from this to the road there without having a spell—from the chest that was from. Never had me breath for a long time. I couldn't work no longer. I used to have to take five or six spells from where we parked the car up to what we call the Dry House. Then when I would get there, there was no use speaking to me, I wouldn't have enough breath to be talking to you anyway. So one night we were there in the mine I had to walk up from the four hundred feet to the other level. I just got in over the landing and I said to Slaney, "That's it for me. One of those days I'm going to go back the other way trying to get up there and be killed. I'm going to quit this altogether." I got me holidays and never went back.

There was no such thing as dust or radiation then, but that's what it was. Everyone that had anything like that, it was "TB". We wouldn't know nothing about it sure, only for Dr. Quinlan, that's who told us about this. We all supposed we had the TB when we had a bad X-Ray. He had us over there in the Hall one day and told us the whole yarn. The graveyard was filled up with people after dying. He wasn't here very long after he told either; they weren't long getting rid of he. But they knowed that all the time. Even the priest knowed it. He made the graveyard bigger. *What'd he make it bigger for?*

73

The Doctor told us all about it anyway. He told us about a place where there was another mine one time, and they all died of the same thing. Sure first when it started up here there was one old fellow up from the States and he says, "St. Lawrence is going to be a wealthy little place after a while, but it's not going to be a very healthy place." He said they'd die like sheep and so they did. There used to be one of them big trucks, stake bodies we called them, whole full of me shift going to Iron Springs. And I can't figure out one man worked with me around now. They're all dead. One of them big trucks. All gone in the graveyard. They went there pretty young too, some of them. In their thirties.

In another twenty years it'll be the same thing, there'll be another bunch like us. Me and me brother was in the hospital one time with Uncle Jack, the three of us hanging onto life. And there was a young fellow up at the other end of the ward, he was working in the mine too. Dr. Hollywood said, "Look John, look at them three men and take an example of what they're like. Now me son, get out of the mine, because in another twenty years you'll be the same thing." The fellow never went back in the mine after. He done the right thing too. The three of us was there dying. Me brother, he was in there screened off taking cobalt, and Uncle Jack, they sent him into hospital the other day.

Me brother, he's got Lung Cancer. But he seems to be better than me with regard to getting around. He goes for a ride every day. That's more than I can do. Bob Kelly, he took this cobalt and he could run a mile. He was playing football. If I could walk two or three times the length of the building, I'd be on top of the world. I wouldn't be able to run twenty yards down hill if the devil was after me. I'd have to lose me life, I wouldn't be able to run to get clear of him.

Now last night I had a tough night again. I thought I was going to smother. I was up the whole night; couldn't even kneel down like I does here. Sat up the whole night at the table. Twasn't so bad all the winter because Channel 10 was on all the winter. I used to watch that, but that goes off now same as the other station. Got nothing to do now, just watch out the window at whatever's going on. There's cars going about here all night long. Pretty well any hour of the night you see somebody going up or down the road.

The sweats is bad lately boy. The whole winter I was like it. I often froze to death with the sweat running out of me head and dropping on the floor. No matter how cold it was, I often near froze to death, clear of me head. I suppose it's from smothering so much, working hard trying to get me breath. I know I had an awful sore stomach, always paining; it was so hard for me to breathe that the muscles all sprained up in me stomach. Me brother, he's the same way. The nurses tell me they change a thousand times a night. They used to have to do that with me when I was down there. When I went in to the hospital the other day, I weighed 201 pounds. When I came out I weighed 180. They took eleven pound off first when I went in there, that was only fluid and water. They were taking water away from me, using some kind of needles and capsules.

I can't stir. Let me up and get out of the house and that's enough, I'm right gone then. I'll tell you what I done the whole winter; I knelt down here on the floor leaning over the chair, the only way I could get any comfort. I'd be there when they go to bed, and time for them to go to school, I be still there. I wouldn't be asleep. I can't understand it. I'd only doze off; that was the only sleep I got all winter. In the hospital I could lie down very good and go to sleep, but the kind of beds we got, they right strain you. Them beds they got there, when you puts them up with that winch and they're up on a slant, they's why you can lie down on them. I can go to sleep on that.

The only place I could doze off at all was here like this. I'd go to sleep and when I'd wake I'd be almost all in, smothered. I'd be so weak I'd be near smothering. I didn't have strength enough to get up out of it. Once you gets straightened up you'd be all right. Two or three times there I didn't think I was getting up at all, I was smothering right there. Then I got afraid, turned the light off, and sat down in the dark there by the table, watching everything going on. Not much went on there the winter time I didn't know about, I'll tell you.

I watches TV till I'm sick and tired. All winter that used to be on all night. I been watching that so long. Day time I can't get my breath at all. Only for that it wouldn't be so bad. I can't walk at all, only from here to the table in the kitchen. I bring the car up as close to the door as I can; not very often I went anywhere in her.

You sit up here four or five months with no one to talk to. I don't go nowhere. I could go up to the Club. I'd spend hours there with just one bottle of beer, having a yarn like you and me are having now to pass away the time. I can't even do that now. I went up there the other evening, to go down to the harbour, see what's going on, see what's doing with the salmon. I never seen nobody. I drove down alongside of the door at Bud's Place; "I must go in here," I says, "and have a yarn with them." I went in. Nobody there. One fellow belong to Lawn just leaving to go when I went in. So he sat down and stayed a little while with me. I had a bottle of beer. He stayed there, this fellow. When he left, that was it, there was no one else to talk to. I went out, and by Jesus I had to get Bud to turn around the car for me. I was right gone for breath, just walking in and out of there. So I'd never get into one of the other Clubs with the old big stairs. You're the first fellow I seen since.

I used to like going to them Times; you know, the scattered Times they has in them Clubs. Sat down and you had a scattered bottle of beer and watch what was going on. I never got near one this year. I was asked out to a few weddings this year and I never got to one. I stay home. I can't go nowhere with that water trouble; perhaps just the time I want to get into the toilet, there'll be somebody in there, three or four in there. Once when I went in St. John's, the Brownstone Hotel, I went right foolish there one morning: they were there lined up, I couldn't get in. So you know what I had to do? I couldn't hold the dropping. I had clothes in the suitcase and I had a big suit of this underwear, and that's what I done, I done it in that. It was dropping out of me into that, it got right soaking. I threw it away, that suitcase, throw it over the wharf when it got dark. No sir, you can't hold it and that's it. Sometimes I'll be in there and fellow'll be knocking on the door, asking me, "What happened? You dying in there?" I be in there so long I couldn't get out of it. If I did leave the toilet to come over, I couldn't stop, it'd be still dropping out of me when I come over to open up the door. I'd let the scattered fellow in and explain, tell him what was wrong. If that ever cut off on me altogether, I don't think Dr. Hollywood could help it. The Doctor told me they made a false passage up through me. He said, "That'll gradually close up on you."

I been here fighting for breath, didn't think I was going to go on. They can't cure me, I knows that. I knows I'm finished. I was expecting to be gone the spring. And I don't think I'll get through next winter. That's the feeling I got; I won't live out next winter.

Because every other year I used to start to get a bit better in the spring of the year. I'd get down around the beach and out fooling around in the dory. But there's nothing like that this year at all; it didn't make no difference to me. I went out there a couple times, went out on the stage and I like to died getting back to the car. Well you can't do nothing like that, can you? No, I don't expect to live too long more, I'll tell you the truth. I'm after telling them, they knows. If next winter be like this winter, I can't see how I can. Isn't anything they can add on to it any worse. This winter I sat up at the table the whole winter; couldn't go lie down and have a nap or anything like that. And with this water trouble I got, I can't see how I can stand it any longer. Although to look at me and talk to me, you wouldn't say there was anything wrong with me, would you? I can't put on me own boots, can't dress meself or nothing.

I got no future whatever left ahead of me. The way I got it sized up, I don't want anything for meself. All I'm looking forward to now is dying. I knows I'm not going to live too long anymore now anyway. However long it is, it's not going to be very long. I'm not going to get next winter out of it. I had it really give up altogether a while ago. Didn't think I'd finish this winter, I thought I'd be gone before the spring of the year come. But I got no thoughts of getting better, of getting well enough to get around.

I wasn't allowed to work, but I used to go out in the dory, jig a bit of fish, put out a couple salmon nets and look after them. Everyone was at me not to go at it; first when I got married to her, she wanted me to sell the boat and fishing gear. I'll never do that no more. Won't be able. All that's gone. I'll never do that no more. I wants to do it, *wants* to do it right now. I feels like going out right now and carrying a couple salmon nets. Me and the brother-in-law had a couple salmon nets. This year I went down, I got halfway over to the dory, but I couldn't even get over the stage head. I just got up to the car and Jesus, I was all in. I still hang on to the dory, a couple nets, the old stage and that. I promised to give it all to me son that's married. I guess one of these days I will; I'll never use it no more.

But I think I'd sooner be dead. Old Tommy Chambers down there, the last words he said when he was dying was, "*Fish! Fish!*"[2]

[2] Mr. Andrews died in March of 1975.

7

The best time ever
I had was mining

*KEVIN KINSELLA: Merchant mariner and rum
runner, street brawler and boxer. Tatooed and
bearded, he looks the reincarnation of all the pirates
who filled one's childhood fantasies.*

We were up at the bar drinking up, me and the boys, when the
door busted out and about three or four hundred coloured guys—
they had cans, they had drums, they had pipes—well, one of the
guys grabbed me, slung me across his back and started carrying me
all across the bar with me on his shoulders. VJ Day. Down in the
West Indies. Eight o'clock at night we got the news. Oh, we had a
lot of fun. It was good country, I like it real well. Everything on
the house for three days. Never had to pay for a drink: cigarettes,
whiskey, everything free. It didn't cost that much anyway, maybe
you'd pay seven cents for that Demerara Rum.

I had that shoulder from the Garden Party racket that come off
up in Lorries. We played that French team that evening, football;
we beat the Frenchmen three to one. They always had lots of
liquor them times. The French guys come in with a crock each and
we'd get together, everybody drink up. So we decided to go to
Lorries to the Garden Party. We went up to Lorries and I went up
to the Hall to look for me old man. I met this fellow on the door,
and he said, "You're not allowed in, you're drunk." I said, "I
can't help that, I want to go in to the Hall and I can't see any

reason why I can't." "Oh no you're not," he said, "I'm Floormaster here." "I don't care if you're Harbour Master, I'm going in and that's it." So we argued and argued. I said, "If you wants to settle this up, there's only one way to do it, come on outdoors." A big man too, about 260. I never weighed more than 160 in me life. No trouble to handle him, he was awkward. He can't slew around that fast, he hasn't got the moves at all. A slimmer fellow's got the quickness. It's only if the big guy hits you, that's it, you'll feel the effect of it. But lots of times he'll hit you and you're going away with it; he won't hurt you, you're going away with the blow.

Feetwork is all of it, that's half the battle. You move in, move out. I know a hundred times that night if he hit me I'd have moved across to the next one. A fist on him as big as that briefcase. Everytime he hit, I wasn't there, and he'd come back and I'd be behind him. I move right around, back and forth, in and out, and he doesn't know what was going on. I almost had him hypnotized. If he got ahold of you, that was it, there was nothing you could do with a man that size. He bit: whatever his mouth could take out of the shoulder, about the size of a fifty cent piece, come out. Savage that was. But he just couldn't hold on to me. I was too much sweaty with just the bare flesh, my shirt ripped off. Oh I had a lot of fun out of that.

About 140 of us from home went down to St. Pierre to play soccer one time. So this boxer, he cleaned up three fellows off a dragger from France, pretty good sparring partners too. I thought, "He's not getting away with that." At the last of it though, they couldn't get no one else to go up with him. I was half drunked up, so I said I'm going to take him on. Me sister says, "No, he'll kill you." "He might kill me," I said, "but not that easy." I went down to the manager and asked did he want a partner, and he said yes. So I went down and they had no boxing shoes to give me, so I said okay, the stocking feet will do me. They asked me what kind of glove I wanted, and I said, "I don't know, ask him." He settled for a six ounce glove, that's a knock out glove eh, no protection at all. He asked me, "How many rounds do you want?" and I said, "I don't care if he fights for a week, I got lots of wind." He settled for fifteen rounds.

Second round they had to stop the fight. I came at him so fast he didn't know where it come from. Caught him right quick. He never had the moves I had. He had the speed to come in but none to get out. He was boxing right handed and I was boxing left and right; I was changing me style and he wasn't. I'd catch him with the left hook all the time; he didn't know where it was coming from, see. If I hit him once with the left hand, I'd hit him fifty times, like the piston of a hand, that's the way I'd hit him. I'd move right, then I'd move left. That's when I caught him. He should have come in with the left hand up, he could have blocked it all. He didn't know the difference, although he was a good boxer. I met him the next morning, and his whole face was almost as black as this, his cheekbones, his two eyes. He looks after the jail in St. Pierre ever since.

I was there that time they beat up Halifax, V.E. Day. That was a bad time. They asked for that, eh? The base at Halifax was all full of every kind of ship, five or six hundred of them, all tied side by side. So the news come in, sirens going. It was pretty good all that day. Next day they barred the liquor stores. Wouldn't give them no liquor, no beer, no nothing. Everything was closed. So they asked for it. We come in town about twelve o'clock, and the Navy was after breaking loose from the barracks. About five hundred of them come down and they raided Buckingham Liquor Store, that was the first place they broke in. They beat that right out. Everybody took what they wanted. About three o'clock in the morning we joined in them. Thousands of liquor everywhere all over the street; there were cases and bottles and whatever you wanted to take. That went on for two days. They went down and raided all the liquor stores; and the last time, they raided the brewery on Water Street, maybe sixteen hundred people then, Air Force, Navy, Army. Everyone got into it; there was so much liquor on the go, everybody joined in. The last thing they done they started raiding the town, they went from one end of Barrack Street to the other and never left one window. Cleaned them all right out and took whatever was in the building and hauled it out onto the street. Oh what a mess.

They went right haywire with no liquor. They figured they were entitled to it, eh? You take a fellow that's been overseas five or six years; then the war's over and you bar off the liquor! The police couldn't do nothing. The police joined in at the last of it. I wouldn't doubt but that there's two cops serving time for that yet. I had fifteen cases of gin meself at the time; you just bring one case aboard at a time from the liquor store. That was marvellous, I guarantee you. Everyone who went ashore come back with five or six suits, a suitcase full of jewellery; whatever you want, you took it. Then they started setting fire to the town. They burned almost half of Barrack Street. After that, they put Martial Law on Halifax, no one allowed on the street after eight o'clock at night.

The Wireless Operator aboard ship, he was a bad one. He had a little dog, and every time I come out of the mess room, the dog used to nip my heel. This evening I was coming out and he was up on the Bridge. I didn't know he seen me. The little dog come for me and I kicked him, went right over the rail he did. A little Bull Terrier he was. Well, we got into it. Twas an awful fight, almost two hours at that. Old Man had to come down and stop us. I didn't know who was the worst of us. We were neither one in very good shape when we knocked off. Kicked him right over the rail I did, the bastard; he wouldn't nip me no more. Oh, we had some awful fun aboard her boy. It was some mixed up crew; Estonians, Norwegians, Brazils.

The best time was in the West Indies and Cuba. I call that God's Country. The people are nice; you go from one house to another, when you went in there you were their friend just the same as all your lifetime. I never saw people like that before. And then every day the sun would be on the boil. And no wind, never seen enough wind to blow that lighter out. I was almost too glad when I got out of her, for I thought I'd be killed. I got into a fight with the cops on the wharf. So I figured if I went back again, that's be it. We were trying to smuggle a girl across to the States. They caught us. Her parents were all dead; she was only young, so we were going to bring her to the States to work. We almost had her aboard too. We had her on the gangway and the cops caught us. I think a fellow squealed on us, that's what happened. Five of them, well rigged too; had a double row of bullets, a revolver each side, and a great big slasher. They shouted out, so we stopped then, went back. One fellow took a swing at me buddy. He fired at Ken and I kicked the other fellow. And she started then! The five of them, they slashed me with blackjacks then, I thought they were going to shoot us, but the Old Man, the Skipper, he talked them out of it. They let us go, but told us not to come back no more. I can see that cop—they all dressed in white suits, big panama hats.

I started working when I was thirteen, picking acid at Black Duck, picking the granite out of the 'Spar' for fourteen cents an hour. I couldn't very well keep going to school because I had to go fishing with the old man. I went in the bow of the dory with him when I was just going ten. I couldn't do much hauling but I could manage to bait hooks. When my brother got old enough to do that, I quit and started working.

I worked up there with a sledge hammer, at Aylwards. I worked with them for fourteen cents an hour with a sledge hammer. From seven in the morning till six in the evening. That was back in 1935 or '36, I was nine years old. I could have gone fishing with the old man too; he had nothing to give me, nothing for it, he couldn't give me enough. Living on ground flour most of the time. He was a fisherman all his life, fishing out of Gloucester, Banking. Lunenberg.

I started mining in '47 when I came back from Halifax from the Marines. I stayed there for ten year straight. Then I quit the mine and went on oil tankers, freighters and all that. I figured I'd go back to sea again. Sailed in French boats mostly, although I can't speak one word of French. I can understand quite a bit of French, but speak it, no way. I went mining then for another few years, then I quit the mine and went down to Churchill Falls. I just wanted to try it, see what it was like.

The best time ever I had was mining. I like mining. I really love mining. I wouldn't go at nothing else in the world if it paid money enough for me, that's provided no disease. But this mine in here, I wouldn't go in that, not meself. Too much bangs. I heard too many of them. Not in Churchill Falls; I seen but one blast in Churchill Falls. Me and the boys sat down after we'd finished drilling off, waiting for the time come to blasting. So we're sat down and I see the face turn right white. I said to buddy we'd better move from this over there because that's going to let go pretty soon. When you hear it, it's a click click, you'd better get out of that, you got no business around there. Something's going to happen pretty soon. But this ground here, knew the ground that well I can tell you when to leave and when to stay. It's up to yourself, if you wants to believe me, okay, but if you want to come, come with me because I know what's going to happen. I've seen too much of it. Seventeen years and I've seen a lot of it. There're a whole lot of fellows in St. Lawrence like me with the experience. It's air blasting. Bumps, we call them. You see smoke coming out of the ground just like a volcano. All of a sudden, boom!

I turned over enough rock meself there to make a millionaire out of that Company. They're making a fortune off them, and you're making nothing. The rest of the boys that was with me done the same thing. And all they got was promises. The same ground they're breaking in Salt Cove Brook now, every month they comes out with six or seven hundred bonus. We were doing the same thing at that time. Where did that money go at then? Who was getting that?

Every time you went to get a Medical, they'd just pass you. But Dr. Quinlan, he come in, and after a little while he found out the trouble. Then he called a meeting over at the Union Hall and told the people what was going on. They were sent into St. John's with "TB". Take that lung out and come home. Everybody was dying in the sanitorium with "TB". Eh? When he told the people what was going on, he didn't stay very long, did he? The Company said, "You get out of here." That's the story there. I'll guarantee it, not only me, but all of St. Lawrence'll do that. When the Company found that out, they heaved he out. I knew one doctor was passing miners just like that, even though they was sick—it didn't mean a thing to him. What he was getting, no one knows yet. You'd go in sick and he'd send you on to work. Dr. Quinlan died in St. John's last year; where he is at today, Lord have mercy on him. I hope he's in Heaven. He's the fellow that got the Compensation going, what gave all the money to St. Lawrence. By the time the people knew what was going on, it was too late. Half the miners in the graveyard.

'69 I come home from Churchill Falls. The wife wanted me to stay home, so I got a job with the Company. I went to the Company, go to the Doctor, and the Doctor told me I was a sick man. He said, "You'd better go to bed." I said, "What do you mean, go to bed?" He said, "You're a sick man and don't know it." He looked at me and he looked at the paper and he tore it up and threw it in the wastepaper basket. "Your mining days is over, you've got to go to bed. You're a sick man and don't know it." "Me sick?" I said. "I just come back from Churchill Falls about a week ago."

So he sent me to St. John's. I was there a month and five days in General Hospital before they found the trouble. I took everything a man could take, and they still couldn't find the trouble. The last time they had a camera go down and they had a TV going over. I looked to see it meself. The table was going every angle, up and down, back and forth, and I could see every time they find a spot they'd stop the TV. I spent me birthday in the hospital and on the 28th I come home. They still didn't know what was what then. They knew what was what but they wouldn't tell me.

When I went back in, there was nine doctors. Nine, and one specialist from Cupids, a little tall thin guy. They took me on the bed and screened me off. They experimented on me. This specialist come asked me about me privates, bowel trouble, kidneys and ears and throat—and they're writing down all this. And the specialist says to me, "What's the reason why you wouldn't take surgery?" "Doctor," I said, "surgery's never proved in St. Lawrence yet. I seen about ninety-four of us, and all that surgery; and no proof ever come out of it. For me it wouldn't make sense, but anything else they got in the hospital, I'll take it." He said, "I knew in St. Lawrence you wouldn't take any more surgery."

Next day, another three doctors come up. They wanted me to take surgery. I said "No way." He said, "There's a growth on your lung, but let me take it out and I'll guarantee you're a sound man for the rest of your life." So I said to the doctor, "If you had a four cylinder car and you took one cylinder away, you think that car would work the same way with three as with four? Well, I can't work without one side of me." That stopped him right then and there. "Well," he said, "there's nothing we can do for you now. If you don't want to take that, that's all we can do." "Is there any more treatment beside that?" "Well," he said, "there's cobalt." "Why didn't you tell me that before?" I said. "If you can work with cobalt, why do you want to take me lung out?" So I had him stopped right there.

They come back the next day, and they said, "Mr. Kinsella, we heard you want to sign yourself out of hospital." I said, "No way.

I told the other doctors yesterday I'll take anything clear of surgery —it never worked." So he come back about ten minutes later with me chart. Next morning at ten o'clock I was down taking me first cobalt treatment. I was down there twenty-three days. I used to go back every morning for three minutes.

I was home just about the year I guess. I goes back, getting check ups all the time eh, and they found this lung clouded, just above me heart. It was the same way on this side, only this side was bigger. So they said, "Do you want to take more cobalt?" I said, "Yes boy, whatever you think'll help, I'll take it. If it kills me it kills me, if it cures me it cures me." I took that another twenty-six days. I had no trouble since that. I come out of that pretty good—that was last year. I've had two check ups since then. No problem.

I gets Compensation. I got that in '70. At the first of it, before I got Compensation, I was on Social Assistance. When they found out I was sick, I had to go on Social Assistance before I got Compensation. I was on that over a year. When I got it, they give me five thousand dollars, and the Government took it from me! I was one of the ones they took it from. So I was five years fighting before I got it back. The same day I took the second cobalt treatment, that's the day this come in force, taking the money from the people. Welfare paid me from '69 to '70 when they found me diseased; I had a big family, twenty-one children, I was getting a good welfare. The Compensation gave me $5,485 backtime; the Government turned round and took the works from me. What the Welfare gave me, they turned around and took that back.

It took me five years to get that back. I fought them all in St. John's when I was in hospital. Confederation Building, the Philip Building; statues and everything else. I used to come and check them every day. I never give them no breaks at all, I just kept right on their backs and somebody had to do something pretty soon. I knew that was me money. That crew in the Compensation building, there's fellows in there I'd love to hang. If I had a chance.

That's not a big lot of money now. I got twenty-one children. I was married in '53, had a baby every year, two sets of twins. As far as I'm concerned, I get something for one of them, I get something for them all. Say this one got a pair of boots, well the other one got boots too. No sweat at all, that's the way I looked at it. That's why

I knocked around so much, I couldn't make money enough home. The mine wasn't paying much. I didn't care what I was going to be, I was fit for anything. I didn't care what it was. Go to sea or mining, I didn't care. I quit the mine to go on the boat. If I got on a boat and I made more money mining, I'd go back in the mine again. That was me life you know. I just had to do it. I had no choice.

Half of St. Lawrence is full of dust. Not only St. Lawrence; Burin, Marystown, different places. Lots of people full of dust. Dust never hurt you see; you can live with dust for years and years with no bother over it. But radium turns it to Cancer. You know yourself you haven't got a chance with that.

I don't go to hospital, no way. If I don't know it, I'll live that much longer, that's the way I look at it. I should be good for another twenty year anyway, that's what I got in me mind. But I'd like to keep going. I keeps it off me mind all the time. I keep moving, keep moving, that's all.

I can go into the country, keep it up all day from six in the morning till six in the evening. The man what keeps up with me got to be in good shape. I'm glad to see what shape I'm in, I'm glad to feel the way I do. They'll never cure me, but they helped me for sure.

I'm getting along good so far. I got to thank God for that. I don't know how long I'm going to last; it could be three days, it could be a month. Probably just go out *psssst*! A lot of guys, it went to their heart: they figured they took this, they're going to die just like that. They go in the house and never come out no more. When I took the cobalt, a lot wouldn't take it, afraid it was going to kill them. They wouldn't do it. If I had to, I'd go back and take it again. It'll keep it from spreading. It might spread, but it won't go so fast. I never had a pain or ache, nothing. I'm putting the front of me house next week, I does me own scaffolding. If it's a nice day I go out in the boat, if it's foggy I go shooting.

I never went to sleep last night at all, I was up all night. I painted the kitchen last night, the loft and the walls. Buddy came off work at four o'clock this morning, so I had coffee with him and stayed up till 5:30 waiting for buddy to call me to go out in the boat. He never called so I called him up and went out in the boat. I don't bother with sleep. Maybe I get one hour in a couple, three days. Even aboard the ship, time would come for me watch, they'd knock on me door and I'd be there looking at them. All the time. They never caught me out. No way. I'd go ashore and maybe I'd get two hours sleep in three days.

No way to get me to sleep. No matter how hard I was working underground, it didn't make no difference. When it was time to go gunning, I'd carry me dog and gun and go on shift at eight o'clock. I'd be finished work at four in the morning, I'd walk the hills till dark that evening. Some nights I'd get home in time to get some lunch and go on to work; some nights I'd get an hour's sleep. That's all, seven days a week.

I don't know how long I'm going to last. Don't know for sure yet. I feels perfect. Not perfect, no, with two sides gone. One side isn't so bad. Yeah, I'm pretty lucky so far.

8
You can't blame the Company

ALONZO MALRAUX: At 49, his manic energy supercharges all encounters—his fingers drum, his feet tap, his elbows pound all surfaces, his muscles seem permanently knotted.

I reared meself! I was only a baby when me mother died. Me sisters and brothers, just the children, one bigger than the other. Then after they got big, they left and went away somewhere. The oldest, she wouldn't have been too old, I suppose she was twelve or thirteen, hardly enough to look after the youngsters anyway. I was the baby, I was only two year old. Me grandmother came up to live with us for a spell. She had another daughter and then her daughter got married and she went to live with her daughter. I used to go back and forth there all the time; I used to stay there most of the time meself. The old man came back here in '37, had a little house built up here. Then when the war started he went to war, father did, so I lived with another man and woman. They come to live with me—they had no place of their own, see. I lived with them till I got married meself, and I built this thing.

I got married in '46 and lived here. And I been working ever since. The first time, I went to work in the old Director picking what we used to call acid. Ten cents an hour we used to get. I was only about twelve or thirteen. When I was small, I never had what they got today, I'll tell you. Lots of times I got home with never a bit of bread for me breakfast or never a drop of tea. More than once, I'll guarantee you. Go in somewhere, the next door neighbour, and if they were eating breakfast, they'd give you a slice of bread or something like that, that's all. The old man used to be gone see. And no one there to do nothing. He used to send money, but it wasn't that much at that time and there was no one to look after it. We were only youngsters; get a bit of money and that'd be gone. Yes boy, we went through lots. We were reared up hard. We reared ourselves. Nobody do nothing at all for us.

The old man was here six or seven years, only two of us in the house. I was about fifteen then. He'd go on night shift and I'd be by meself. He was working on the surface, in the Dry House. I used to cook his dinner for him and he cooked mine. Every bit of money I'd get, he'd take from me. I used to get me own cheque and give it to him; if he give me five dollars, well all right, and if he didn't, all right too. He told me he put it away, but I never got it. I never even got the house after he died. That was supposed to be mine because I built it. He died without a will. I never got five cents. Nobody got nothing.

I don't know why. I suppose he was reared up hard hisself and he wanted to do the same with us. You couldn't talk to him. He wouldn't listen. And if you dared give him an answer! I wouldn't give him an answer even after I got married. No sir. Not only me, but neither one of us. If he said you had to do something, you had to do it. His arms were like that; if he hit you he'd split you open. A hard old case he was. He wanted to let you know he was the boss.

Whatever me brothers want, he give them. He never give me nothing. When I went to work in the mine he used to take me cheques. But they never give him nothing. Neither one of them, not five cents. Whatever they wanted, he'd give it to them. If *I* wanted anything! When I came into this house it wasn't even finished, I just had the kitchen and that room there then, and I had an old stove that wouldn't do nothing. And he come in here and he said, "Boy, it's some warm in here." Honest to God, he wouldn't give me a bag of coal. I used to be a bit saucy to him, more so than the rest. I used to tell him about the house; I used to tell him I owned it. He wouldn't have that. I made sure I was far enough away to run, I'm telling you. He didn't like that. But I never got it.

In the Depression, lots of times I come home and there was no one in the house. Perhaps I'd go to the cupboard looking for something to eat and there'd be nothing. I'd take a cup of water and go on again. And then you'd come home that night to go to bed, still nobody home, still nothing in the cupboard for you to eat. Only a bit of bread you'd get from somebody in the day time. I found that hard. Half the time nothing belonging to you, and in your bare feet. But I've had it pretty good since I started work meself. I found it pretty good, thank God—so far.

I went to Argentia then. I was only a young fellow, I was under age. And I was there two weeks before I got on at all. They wouldn't hire on young fellows for labour. The last day I went to him. "Nothing doing," he says. "Sir, if you got the job," I said, "a pickaxe and a shovel don't frighten me. I can do the work." "Do you think so?" he says. "I'm sure of it" "Okay," he said "I'll hire you on." So I got the job and I worked there all winter; outdoor labour, pickaxe and shovel.

I come home then. The manager in the mine, he asked me, "Why don't you go work with us?" So that's where I went, I went in there and worked with them on the surface three or four months. They were short of miners then, and the news got around that young fellows have to go underground or go home, laid off. Jesus, I said, I'm not going home, I'm going underground. So I signed on and went down underground in February '42, and I worked there till '60.

There was no rules or regulations, only the Company's. The Mine Captain or the foreman, they never looked at nothing for safety. Someone had to be killed or hurt or beat up before that thing was done. You could tell them a hundred times before that, but they never bothered about doing it till somebody got hurt. And then all of a sudden it got done. Well sure, why not do it before?

And the mine, oh my God, smoking! If you were over here and I were over there, you wouldn't see a man; you wouldn't see nothing, only just a light on his head. That was like that then for eight hours, twenty-four hours around, 365 days in the year. We didn't mind it you know, you worked away and didn't mind the smoke. Sometimes you'd feel a little dizzy and you'd go out and get a bit of air and have a smoke and go back again.

If you refused something, then you had it. You always had it bad after that. You'd have to watch yourself; everything you'd do then they'd be watching you trying to get something on you to fire you. That's what happened to me the last eight months I went back. They wanted me to go down this place, this manway, and I wouldn't go—I said it was too dangerous. They said I had a choice, I either had to go there, or I had to go home. So I took the choice. I come home. I ne'er ever got back again though. I tried it too, and I never got back. What good's the money if you went down there and got killed? That's the way I looked at it. If you're sixty feet down a little round hole, about half the size of that table, and sixty feet above you were big slabs; if one of them big slabs falls across that big manhole, how are they going to get you? By the time they gets through, there wouldn't be enough left of you to put in a nut box. I wouldn't take no chance, but then I had to come home. No more job. And stay home.

I wasn't getting anything from nobody, only just Able-Bodied Relief in the winter time. I had to go fishing in the summer. I had to take me youngsters' baby bonus and go up to the bank and get a loan to pay a boat to go fishing. I didn't know nothing about fishing. I'd never done no fishing. I had to learn. And I had to buy fishing gear and everything; they used to give you so much each, pay it out of your cheque, whatever you make. They had their first half, they were going to have theirs anyway regardless of what you had. You had to go and get Able-Bodied Relief then. That wasn't very much. We had nine youngsters, meself and the wife, and seventy-five dollars a month we were getting.

In the spring of the year you'd start off, get ready for fishing. The Relieving Officer come; well, you'd go over and get your Order and tell him you're getting ready for fishing. He wouldn't give you a full order then, he'd give you a half. If you didn't get no fish by the time he come back again, he'd give you what he owed you, to make up. Anyhow, we started off, he gives me fifty dollars; we went fishing and we made thirty, sixty dollars for the two of us. And down in Burin, they took so much out of that for their nets; they had their share. When he come again the next month—it was a beautiful morning, and I said to the wife, "I'm not going to stay in from fishing. When he comes you take the receipt, write a note, put it in the envelope, and give it to one of the girls to cart over and give to him. He'll see himself what I'm at." So that's what she done. I went in that evening round five o'clock; had a couple hundred pounds of fish, that's all I had. I come in and asked to see the order. And he never give her a cent, not five cents! Because I made thirty dollars, he said, and he wouldn't give me nothing. And the fish, he said, probably the fish would strike, probably in the week coming. I started cursing and swearing!

At the time another Relieving Officer was going round about something, and he come into the house. "You looks mad looking," he says. And I says, "Yes, I am mad. Going on two months now I got to keep nine youngsters, meself and the wife on fifty dollars. I sent over today for to get my Order and buddy wouldn't give me no one." So he never stopped at all. He said, "If I can find him, I'll find him and find out what's going on." So he went out. He called Burin, everywhere, couldn't get hold to him. So it was about eleven o'clock that night he come back, he said, "Mr. Malraux, I'm sorry. I called Burin, and I went to Little St. Lawrence, but I couldn't get ahold to him. But if I can get ahold to him tomorrow, I'm going to find out what's going on."

Well I never heard nothing. The next morning I went meself, I carried the receipts over, and there was another one, another Relieving Officer. He looked at the books and he says, "You wasn't here last month, you never got nothing last month." "I know," I says, "not that I wasn't here though, I was here." And he said, "What happened?" "Well," I says, "you see that thirty dollars here? I made that. I didn't come meself because it was a good day fishing and I didn't want to lose a good day's fishing. So I sent this over to him so he could see, and he never give me no one. He wouldn't give me what he owed me from the last month and he wouldn't give me for the month coming up." He said, "He wasn't allowed to do that with you. If you did make thirty dollars, you were allowed to make thirty dollars. And you could do what you liked with that thirty dollars. He couldn't keep your Order from you. Now I don't mean to say now you could go out and drink it," he said, "or waste it. But you could buy clothes for your youngsters, or buy something to put in your home." And I said, "Sir, that's what he done." Buddy turned around and gave two cheques to me. So he could do what the other fellow wouldn't do.

I quit fishing in '67. Short breathed, see. Not like I am now, but short breathed. When I worked I used to find pain through the shoulder: I used to have to lie down when I come in from fishing. I used to be right gone, wouldn't know what way to put meself in the night time; me arms and everything else were paining that much, no way for comfort.

In the spring of '67, I got a job with Tarefare. They were sinking a shaft over at Tarefare, and there was good money in it. I was making around four or five hundred dollars for every two weeks, with bonus and all. I got a chance to go, so I went there. I never went to no doctor or nothing. I figured if I got a few months at it, it'd put me through and then probably I could knock off and go fishing again. I only worked two weeks. Had to give it up. I used to pass blood. If I'd get wet, I used to pass blood. I went in to the Doctor then, and I told him and I said, "Doctor, I've got a job but I've got to give it up."

"Well," he said, "where're you working at?" I said, "I'm working over at Tarefare digging the shaft." And he said, "Who told you to go over there?" And I said, "I told meself." He said, "You know you're not allowed to work in the mine." I said, "Yes. I got nine youngsters too. They're going to school and there's nothing to give them to eat neither, hardly. I figured I'd work there and get a few months, then I'd go back to fishing again. Apparently I can't do it. When I gets wet, I passes blood." He said, "Well you're not going back no more." "No, I know I'm not."

"Well now," I said, "what about giving me a Paper for when the Relieving Officer comes so he can give me something, something to help me get some fuel to burn. There's no way I can get something to burn without going three or four miles to bring wood in on me back, and I can't do that." He said, "No, you can't do that. When he comes, you ask him for a Paper, and when you gets the Paper, you bring it in to me and I'll fill it out for you." I said, "No, that's not going to work." I said, "You give me a Paper and I'll carry it to him and he'll give me a Paper, then I'll bring it back to you." "Oh no," he said, "you go on."

So when the R.O. come, I went. I went in to him and said, "I been to the Doctor the other day and he turned me down from the mine, he turned me down flat. Also he told me to get a Paper from you." He said, "I can't do that; you get the Paper and bring it to me." So I said, "Well sir, that's what the man told me. If you thinks I'm telling you a lie, you takes the phone and you call him

93

and ask him." And that's what he done. He said, "Doctor, there's a man here named Malraux. He tells me you told him you turned him down a week or so, and told him to ask me for a Paper. I can't do that unless you give me a Paper."

And the Doctor says, "No, I did not tell him." The Relieving Officer reaches over to me and said, "He tells me that he never told you." I said, "You tell him he's a goddamn liar. I don't care if he hears it or not. What he didn't tell me, I wouldn't tell you." Well he wouldn't give me that Paper, first to last. I had to go on Social Assistance.

They wouldn't turn me down, see? The Doctors and everything else, they're getting paid for it, eh? I mean the Company knew what was going on in there, the Doctors knew. But the people didn't know it was there. And everything was covered up; do you understand? You had to be dying before they'd really turn you down, and say you were disabled. They wouldn't let you go underground, but they'd pass you for to go to work.

A while after, there was a football game on. The Doctor was down there lying over the fence. When the first half was over, I went down to talk to him. He said, "How're you feeling, 'Lonzo?" I said, "Pretty good, Doctor, sometimes; but more times I'm not. I'd like to know what time I can go in and get an X-Ray off of you. I'd like to have an X-Ray, because in two weeks time I'm going in to St. John's, and I'm going to get a lawyer." He said, "I'll send for you." So I waited and all September come and went, and still no call. I went in meself. I told buddy I wanted to see the Doctor. "No way, you won't see the Doctor today." You know, I stayed there two hours and never got to see him. So I come home. He calls me then, and I went right in. Sure enough, he carted me upstairs and give me X-Rays.

"You stay there," he says, "till I calls you." I sat down and waited, and he called me in. "Alonzo," he said, "you want my opinion, don't you?" I said, "Yes, I don't care what it is, you're not going to frighten me. I got an idea what I got, so you needn't be a bit afeared to tell me." "Well boy," he said, "you got dust on your lungs. You got no cancer yet, but you got dust. I'm going to phone in to the Compensation for you."

Two or three weeks after, I gets a call, have to go in to St. John's. So I went to St. John's and had to go see Dr. Creighton.

Dr. Creighton signed me in and gave me a complete going over, and he said, "Mr. Malraux, you got dust on your lungs. I can't tell you whether you're going to get anything or not because we got so many doctors; you have to go through so many that I can't tell you. But I think that you'll get some. I can guarantee you that you'll get some. How much they'll give you, I don't know. You can go home," he said, "and probably the Board'll want to see you. You don't have to come back to me no more."

So next day then up at the Board. They send me back to the boarding house. I was down at the boarding house three weeks waiting for a call from them, for what they were going to tell me. I was feared to go out anywhere, feared I'd be gone when they call me. If I went downtown, I'd want to go and get back as quick as I could. After a while I got dirty. The taxi driver used to come down to the boarding house every morning to pick up the patients to carry to hospital. I went to him this morning and I said, "Listen me son, when you goes back you tell them to send me down a pass. I wants to go home out of this. That's long enough here. You tell them 'Lonzo wants to go home." Sure enough, when he come down that evening he had a pass. And I come home and I still didn't know nothing. Never knew a thing.

After Christmas, I got a cheque. Eighty dollars it was, I think. No, fifty. I was turned down 50%. I got fifty dollars a month. I got a letter with it; 50% disabled. So then I started getting me cheques. During that summer I gets a call to go back up to St. John's again. I had Cancer. Cancer of the lung. In the winter I was 50%, and then in the summer I was 100%, just as quick as that. In a few months. They found it in the spit—I was after going in here and taking the spit test, and they sent it to St. John's. In order for me to get me full Compensation, I had to take cobalt treatment. If I didn't take it, I wouldn't get no Compensation out of it yet. They didn't tell me I *had* to take it; it was up to meself, eh? But if I didn't take it I wouldn't get no more Compensation. They wanted to take the lung out: I wouldn't take the lung out. So then they come back with the cobalt treatment. I said I'd take that.

Uncle Pat Duff, they give him too much cobalt. They burned him up like a scruncheon. They blasted too much at first and it burnt. But they didn't do that to me see. Me chest is the same when I come home as when I went. A little mark there yes, like a tattoo, that's all it is. Sick? I was sicker than a dog for about a week or so. They give me a paper in case I broke out in a rash, telling me what to do with meself. If you takes cobalt and you breaks out in sores after, you're not cured. But if it don't break out in sores, well they finds you cured. I didn't break out, no pimples or nothing. That proved that if there was anything there, they cured it. Same with Kevin, he never broke out. But poor old Gus Reardon, he broke out in sores. He wasn't fit to look at. I knew then he wasn't cured. I could have told him then, but I wouldn't tell him. He's dead a year or so after he took cobalt.

I'm not cured. Me right lung is going see. This is what I can't understand, why they wouldn't give it to me. They give it to Kev Kinsella on both lungs, so what way couldn't they give it to me? Dr. Hollywood sent me in for to take it, but Dr. Rourke, he told me he wouldn't give it to me because if he did, I'd be a cripple for the rest of me life. I don't know if he only just told me that because I wouldn't have the operation or what. Probably he wanted to give the operation. Me right lung is infected and spreading. They gave me $250. Live on that the rest of me life, no matter how high the cost of living goes.

I look good. If I wasn't spitting up blood now, I'd say yes, I've got a good chance. I be spitting up blood since I come out of hospital, every day. I looks the best kind. I eats good too. The Doctor said it's good for a little while yet, not too long. I figured then he only give me a year. But I knows I'm getting worse. I can tell meself, with the breath, and the pains I has now. I has pains through the chest I never has before. And spitting up this blood, and this burning there in me stomach. And I don't have to walk at all, just lay down on the day bed—and this'll grab me like cutting off the breath. You can't go by a man's looks. After I came home from St. John's, they figured there was nothing wrong with me because I looked so good. You might be the healthiest kind to look at: that person, he might in a month's time be in the grave-yard.

I don't do nothing now. I just go along in the car, that's all. Roaming around, back and forth to Marystown, up and down the Shore. Trouting; I can't even do that this year. Every other year I'd go out fishing; me and her would go up, and the youngsters, go up to Lamaline trouting. But this year I can't get out at all. I stay here home most of the time. I don't go to no Clubs, she don't go to no Bingos; there's no money to do it. When you can't work, that's it, it's finished.

I know I'm dying, and she knows I'm dying, so there's not much future for either one of us now. No future at all now. It's in the past. You sit down and you know one of those days you're going to pass out. That's all. That's the only future here.

There's nowhere to go here see, clear of Clubs—I can't afford to go to Clubs. Nowhere to go to pass away an hour. Now last year, and the year before, we used to go to the Stella Maris. We used to play nickel games, five cents a game. We used to spend all day and all night just to pass the time. Bill Fitzpatrick and a bunch of the older fellows'd get together. Sit down and talk to your buddy, another fellow just like you. But since Bill died, there's none of that. He died the same, the Cancer, he worked down there when they first started off. People cut it out see, because he brought it on. He started it off, then we all got interested in it. All at the table, get together. You'd be right back again after supper till it closed at twelve o'clock at night. You'd have a bottle of beer or something, that's all. You wouldn't win nothing and you wouldn't lose nothing; you wouldn't lose nothing even if you did lose, fifty cents in a day. It was a great pastime. I always used to look for it. Every day you'd be waiting till the time come to go. But now there's no one there. No one to go, no one to talk to. You might meet one or two others during the day, that's about all; you only come back to the house again.

You can't get people together at all. You can't get no one in the one world to do anything. That's why you'll never get nothing. I don't know why that is, it was always like that here. They're begrudging, only begrudging the other fellow what he gets. He figures I'm getting ten, twenty dollars more than him, he's begruding that. If there's any way he can get that from me, he's going to take it. So that's what's going on. Everybody's for theirselves. The more they can get, the better for theirselves. Compensation's the same way. You no way can't get together for to go in to St. John's and say, "Now boy, look, the cost of living's gone up and I'm not getting money enough." You can't get nobody to do nothing, can't get them together. I tried it.

Most of them see are only turned down 30%. They're getting

their Compensation and they're working besides, making very good money. You know, they're not worrying, eh? They're not worrying about me or someone else. When I was a young fellow working in Salt Cove Brook, if a man got sick we'd make a collection—a man that was turned down and wouldn't be able to work. We'd all go over and make a collection, give whatever we could, five or ten dollars. There was no Compensation then. Then they cut that out. A man gets sick, a man comes home, and that's it: no such thing as anyone trying to help you out. No, I never got five cents for it, not even from the Company, and I worked thirteen years in the mine. For all the hard work! I used to work Sundays and everything, twenty-four hours a day underground sometimes.

I don't owe nobody nothing. I reared the youngsters good, thank God. They're all good to me, every one of them. If they get up and get a job, they all sends the money to help me out. So I got no regrets. The youngsters never done what they like. I kept them down, I reared them more or less like I was reared meself. I'm the boss, and you go and come when I tell you. I never let them out in the night time; dark come and I know where they're to. They wanted to go all right, but the time come to be in and they'd be in, or I'd be looking. I never had no trouble. If I only had the last dollar, I'd give it to them. I wouldn't see them hungry for nothing. If I got it, they're going to get it. I loves the youngsters. I wouldn't like to see anything happen to them. I never had to lay me hand on them once, not once.

I know what I've got wrong and I don't care. I got the lung burned out and I'm not worrying about it. I don't know when . . . but I'd like to have another three years anyway. But if I got to go, that's it. I'm not going to worry. If He wants me to die, well, there's nothing I can do about it. So long as all the youngsters are happy, I'm not going to worry about it. It's no good to worry. If you starts to worry about it, you're finished, you're gone. I mean I knows what I got. If I lives another year, well all right, and if I don't, God's Will. I wouldn't want to die sudden: I'd like to know I'm going to die and get to see everybody. I thought I was going to die last year, and I wouldn't get to see them—I worries about the youngsters, always.

I'll be fifty on Saturday. And they'll all call in on Saturday, from St. Pierre and Toronto. They thinks the world of me, the youngsters, and I thinks the world of them. I was off work all right, but there was never a great hunger because I done everything. I used to get enough to keep the table going. I went fishing, and if I'd get an extra hundred dollars I'd go to St. Pierre and get the liquor, come home and go bootlegging. I'd sell a drop of liquor and do a bit of mining, to put us through the winter time. And get a bit of extras, a bit of extra clothes for the youngsters. They were never what you call hungry: they had lots to eat and lots to wear. That's all I could do. If they could have had more I would have give it to them; but they knew they couldn't get it, so they didn't bother. They didn't go wearing no dirt or rags, they always kept clean. Yes, I'm very proud of the youngsters I'll tell you. And there's always a place for them; if ever they wants to come home, come and stay as long as they like. That's why I wants everything to go to them when I dies.

You can't very well blame the Company, I suppose. They owns the job, they're not going to tell me what's there, probably close down the mine. They're going to keep that mine going as long as they can. You can't blame the Company. It's the people that runs it I would blame, foremans and Mine Captains. They're the ones to blame. They're doing there, they know what's going on; the Manager, he don't know what's going on, he's up on the surface. You had to watch out for yourself underground. The Mine Captain wouldn't tell you, the foreman wouldn't tell you—he'd encourage you to go there, that's all. And if you didn't go, you had to go home. One way or the other.[3]

[3] Mr. Malraux died in January of 1975

9

I'm the man and the woman since he got sick

*PAUL and WANDA DUFF: Famed for once wrestling a Mountie for his billy club and winning, Paul seems broken by his ordeal in the mines. It is Wanda who must now give order to their lives. Both man and wife tell their stories below.**

He's getting used to it since he been turned down in '69. But I tell you it was some hard to get adjusted to it at first. He called in and I said, "I hope you have got TB, cause there's a cure for TB." It was hard first. The first two years he came off, he was like a man come out of the Mental. He was at the window, door, he couldn't adjust hisself. For thirty years he worked, he couldn't adjust. Well, right on the back of them two years he had a nervous breakdown. Cause he was never used to being home. But after that, he begin to make up his mind it's good to be alive, eh? I mean, me God there's a lot gone that came off after he came off. He don't drink, he don't take in any kind of enjoyment—only just if we went down to our son's for an evening, that's all. He don't upset hisself. That is a help.

I wouldn't be able to tell you how many thousands of pills he's after having since '69. Well there's so much in his system now that it comes out in his underwear; when you take off his underwear to wash it, it's the colour of the drug, and that's really a fact. I mean

* Paul's words are italicised

he's really looking after hisself. If anything happens to him, it's not that he neglected hisself.

There's a certain time in the morning, eight o'clock shift would come, eh? Eight o'clock in the morning. I was supposed to go to work at eight o'clock! Well, I figured to meself, that time I'd go over to the window pane; trying to make yourself think, you know, think that you were clocked off and not allowed to go to work. Four o'clock it'd be the same thing, because they used to work three shifts round. I finally got adjusted to it at last. I haven't been into the Brook after that, although I've got many invitations from the Company to go back and visit the mine . . . because I knew all the bosses and that there. I've become a Life Member of the Club, the Newfluor Club, the Staff Club. We were made members of that; any fellow what had over twenty-five years service to the Company. I had twenty-five years service in '65 see, so I got the pin and the watch from the Company. She been on me arm now since they give her to me . . . she's aluminum.

This blower here is all that keeps him alive now. In the night I've got so used to this. It's just the same as death in the bedroom because he's using that five or six or seven or eight times in the night. His breath cuts right off. Say he's going to St. John's, or going to Marystown, he's got to put that in his pocket and carry it with him.

He's no good for trouble now, not Dad. I'm the man and the woman since he got sick. I got to be man and woman because if anything at all turns up, he's just right useless. If he has to correct one of them youngsters about something, he has to go up and fall on the bed. And the daughter here, she come out for Easter, she had her Easter Holidays home and we had a ball. She went back Easter Sunday afternoon, and Monday morning she was put in the Mental, up on the Psychiatric Ward. She was there eight weeks. I made two trips and Dad made one trip in over the road. I'm telling you that I just about went to pieces meself. She's just identical to me, and anything in the God's earthly world she could do for you. Well, like me, anything I can do for anyone: deaths, anyone dies, knock on the door, come on they're dying, and I'll be gone for two or three days. Washes them meself, lays them out, puts them in the casket, stays till they're buried. And Mary's the same. To think she would go like that. She didn't know her dad, didn't know me.

Me father was born in 1860 and married in 1894; that's the year he built this house. This house was cut in the country and sawed by hand. It's warm; all you need in the winter time is a couple space heaters, that's all, and the range in the kitchen. Me father was a very quiet man. He used to play the flute. . . .
He was only thirteen when his father died. He come out of school then. He had to be the man then, you know, to take that responsibility. He had six or eight in the family.

I didn't seem to mind it somehow. I had me health then. I could walk and didn't mind it; keep the cattle, keep everything going, milk and butter on the table. I kept two cows all the time. The brother in the States, he knew the conditions was home here, and when he had the five dollar bill, the ten dollar, he always wrote home and he always put it in the envelope. When things was getting pretty shy, the ten dollar bill fitted right in there.

I was twelve year old when I went fishing. We fished from home, dory fishing we called it. You'd go out and fish all day, and return in the evening, split and do it up. You fished then from May till around October. The weather was getting pretty rough on this coast the last of October; well, you'd quit fishing. Then you went back to the woods and cut wood for fuel, and also to cut material for to keep up our fishing premises. When the snow come then, we started to haul our material. And then you raised your cattle, you cultivated your ground; we used to have a couple milk cows, and an ox for hauling wood. And in between during the winter months you'd be mending up your nets and knitting up twine in the night. When the spring would break you'd go back to the soil and manure the land and cultivate the vegetable gardens. And then by that time the herring would be moving in and that'd be the first of the fisheries. You'd start with the herring, then you'd fish right on to the caplin, then the squid, and then right on through. And then right around again to the next year.

I tried to do it all. I fished with different men. At that time the Nova Scotia vessels used to come down: that was before Confederation, and they weren't allowed to take any bait in Newfoundland themselves. They hired what they called a Bait Hauler. Now Mr. Lake next door, he used to be a seine man, a Bait Hauler, had his

*own seine net; and I'd go with him, go haul bait. You'd make
eighty dollars a vessel; probably that'd last about three weeks,
probably get six or eight vessels before they'd all be gone. Then
he'd pay us off; I'd get about $150. That was pretty good then, I
mean with the help of a few fish I got besides in the trap, you made
up a fairly good summer. If you made around four hundred dollars
them years, it was really good to you because you'd see the price
of everything with it.*

*The best memories back in the young days is Entertainments. I
always used to take part in Entertainments, concerts, you know,
plays. You used to have some good plays around here in them
days; three act plays like* Lighthouse Nan, *and* Pearl the Fishermaiden. *Stories from years gone by. Probably about twelve cast in
it, usually six girls and six boys. We put on a play every month.
That's what we used to spend our time at night time in the winter.
They used to be held in the old hall. It wasn't that expensive, there
wasn't that much costumes bought, you'd make up your own.* The
Path Across the Hill*! Pearl the Fishermaiden was a sea story;
twas a little girl was washed away and washed up on the shore.
She finally . . . people picked her up and reared her and she got
married and settled down after. Really nice plays they were. And
then another one we had was* Ten Nights in a Bar Room. *That was
an anti-drinking play, fighting and everything going on there. I
remembers the little girl now, she used to come to the bar to look
for her father; and her father, he was in a fight with the other guy.
He had the glass in his hand and let go the glass at her father,
missed him, and struck her just as she was coming through the
door. Split her open right across here. She was done up. She had
to come through the door just at that particular time when the
fake glass was thrown. That was back in the early Thirties. We
used to have great fun with that.*

*I have something here, I don't know if you would be interested
in it or not. It dates back to 1935 and it tells you what people used
to live on at that particular time. It came out of the premises of
the late Mr. Victor Turpin, and he at that time used to give out
what they called the dole, the six cents a day racket. When his
store was renovated a few years ago, one of the young fellows
picked up this and supposed I'd be interested in it. Took it and
brought it home to me. And I said, "Son, I'll hold on to that, it's a*

nice thing to have." So this is it, this is the book. This is Mrs. Sarah Flynn now, she had $1.80 a month, I think she had two children. Here's her month's allowance; now look, nineteen pound flour and a gallon of molasses, a pound of tea, five pound of pork, a quarter of a gallon kerosene oil—no electric lights then—and a cake of yeast, and one cake of soap, a pound and a half of sugar. That came to five dollars. That's incredible, isn't it? If you told people when you go back what you saw, they'll hardly believe it.

On November 15th, 1939, I moved over to the Newfoundland Fluorspar Company. There was no work and not much money going, and there was a little bit of money offered in there. I decided to go at that. I started at seventeen and a half cents an hour, we built a road. And I got twenty-five cents underground, two dollars an eight hour shift. We were sinking a shaft then and they were down 150 feet and just broke off the drift to go north and south. So from that then we started, we went fourteen hundred feet on the south end and we went eight hundred feet on the north end. Air conditions was really bad them times. There was times when a match wouldn't burn in the drift. We were inhaling everything then, there was only one ventilation, and that was the shaft.

When we got to the four hundred foot, things began to brighten up a bit, there was more jobs on the surface. So I put in an application for a job on the hoist, a hoistman's job. I went into the hoist house late in 1942. It was just as well as I stayed underground because the compressor was there in the hoist house with you. It was dusty because at that time we had no dry house, and every miner came up with his wet oil clothes; that's where he brought it in and hung it up in the hoist. There was times you couldn't see across the door, and there was times you had to brush off the table to sit down and eat your lunch. Everything that come from underground, I hoisted. I was from '42 to '69 at that, stayed right in the one place, never changed. It was the only job paying any money at that time; whatever they were getting drilling underground, you got up there. And you never had to buy no oil clothes up in the hoister, whereas you had to buy your oil clothes and rubber boots underground—they never stood very long; if you got a month out of a suit of oil clothes you'd be pure lucky.

When me daughter was born in '46, the day that she was born, he was laid off from the Company. He was ditching; and he went to work that morning and the midwife was here, and he was only gone an hour when he come home and he said to me, "The baby's not arrived, but I'm laid off." And I said, "Well that's great news; if the baby do arrive, that's great news." Anyway, we had cattle then and we took one out of the stable and we sold her. Do you know how much we got for her? Ninety-five dollars. Do you know how long we lived on ninety-five dollars? Six months! On ninety-five dollars.

Around '64 I wasn't feeling too good. I didn't mind that, I had a cough and that. I didn't know what it was, to tell you the exact truth. In 1966 I got real bad, went into hospital; got a bad cold, pneumonia. After a month I went back to work again. That was just pneumonia. So in 1968 then I got real bad: I begin to find me breath, short breathed see, couldn't even go up the hill hardly. When I'd be walking against a hill, I'd stop. I wouldn't be able to keep pace with the other fellow. That was the first I knew something was getting wrong with me then. So '68 I went in to hospital, and that time the lungs got real bad. In fact, they almost collapsed. Anyhow, Dr. Hollywood kept me in there and said, "I think I'll send you in to St. John's for special tests."

Doctor came into him and he was going to send him to St. John's that day. I was here that evening. I don't know what I was doing, but I phoned and he said, "Would you be able to come in at seven o'clock, I want to have a talk to you." And of course it hit me right away; I mean when you get that word that they want to have a talk to you, you know there's something they're going to tell you. He said, "I'll meet you in the corridor." So I went. He said, "We'll go down to the operating room and see the X-Ray." So I went down. I said, "Yes Doctor, I was figuring out that, but it won't surprise me." He said, "Mrs. Duff, I'm not going to tell you if it's Radiation or Silicosis, it's not for me to say. But," he says, "I'm very doubtful." He said, "We're going to send he in and have the tests done. But if I could come out and have heart enough to tell you, I'm almost sure what they're going to find." He went in and had the tests done. But it was hard to take the worst of it.

I went in the 27th of March to the Sanitorium. They wanted to determine did I have TB or what did I have. There was some spot on the lung, something Dr. Hollywood seen on the lung there. The following Tuesday the Doctor came up through. He said, "We done the test on you, we found out that you haven't got TB. There's not a sign of TB." Well he never told me from that day to this what I had, honest to God, I'd kiss the book to that. He never said you got Silicosis or anything. It's only what I judged meself from down there. But afterwards I came home here, Dr. Hollywood told me what I had. They released me then, and I came home here. When they found I didn't have TB, there was no more requirements for me in the San; there was no work for me when I didn't have TB.

He called in and I said, "I hope you have got TB. There's a cure for TB."

When I left to go to St. John's, Doctor didn't tell me, but he told the wife. He didn't tell her right out blunt, but he give her enough to know what I had. He didn't tell me. I suppose he was afraid I was going to crack under or something. But I knew what I had because the way we are here, whatever the other fellow dies with, that's what you got. We're all tarred with the one brush, any fellow that went under the collar in there. Just like I told the fellow in St. John's. I said, "Son, look, there's no way of curing that underground. Put whatever you like underground, but you're not curing it unless you get sunshine; and you're not getting no sunshine underground."

I stayed off work two months. And Dr. Hollywood said, "I'll give you a trial Paul, I'll send you back and see what you do." So he sent me back to work. I worked till September. By Jesus, I was feeling rotten. September come, I started losing time. I was sick, eh? Come home every second day sick.

With a big family, he was missing work. He was going to work; probably one week he'd get a full week, the next week he'd get two days. Off for two weeks, come back for another two days. Then probably come off for another week. It was better in the long run to take him off it.

He was so bad then when he was working in there that he fell asleep on the hoist. And he with the care of every miner was down in under that ground. And this foreman said that only for that he knew that he was sick and wouldn't give up, because they wouldn't turn him down—that he could have went and had him fired right off that job. But he came to me and he said, "You'd better take your husband and carry him to the Doctor and tell him that he's fallen asleep in on his work." They would not turn him down. They'd take him in and they'd let him stay there for four days and five days, and they'd give him a slip to go back to work. There's one man up on the hill the same way now. He's just as bad as what me husband is now. And do you think they'll turn him down in there? Not in to the Salt Cove Brook nor the Doctor will not turn that man down. And the man cannot walk. When he gets up in the morning, he got to stand and watch to see can he make the step before he knows whether he's going to walk or fall. And they did the same with me husband. He was just about gone when they turned him down.

So finally I went in and Dr. Hollywood said, "That's enough. I'm going to take you off. You're not able to stand up."

Upset? Yeah. No. I didn't. . . . Well, the way I considered it, it was something come for me, that was it. If I had that, there was no cure for it. Because me sister's son, he had his lung taken out and he only lived eighteen months. I got a touch of Cancer, and the Silicosis included in it. I got to have drugs every single day. I got to have drugs to give me breath. If I was feeling as good inside as I'm looking outside, I'd be all right. I'm not feeling good at all. If you and I left now to walk up the street, I'd have to let you go on. I'd walk at me own pace, because I got to sit down and have a rest.

But thank God. I suppose I consider meself lucky. That's '69 that I'm turned down; there's a lot of me buddies gone under the clay since that. But I'm living right up to what the Doctor tells me, and that's that.

He came back after he got home and got care. You know, he's come back to hisself. He's after putting on weight. He was real thin, but he's after getting fat now—which is not good for him, the Doctor is mad about it. The Doctor scolded him. And even smoking; I tried him with the pipe, but he could never get used to the pipe, and he says, "If I'm going to die with what I got, well smoking won't kill me." So I says, "Tis your health, and tis you. So if you figures out you want to have a smoke, go ahead and have it; cause you're not going to get better. No one was cured of it."

The sunshine makes me feel better. But let the fog close in now and you won't hardly hear me talking. Cut right off her then, right tight. And that's where pretty well all of us got it, that's the way you'll feel. We don't have to have any forecast, us fellows, to tell

107

us what kind of a day we're going to have tomorrow. I can tell her a day in advance—I'll feel that tightening up here, tightening up.

I had a brother in St. Lawrence, he went down and had an operation. He only had about the size of this on one lung—that's my sister's husband—he phoned home and he had twelve doctors around the bed. He phoned home to his wife to have her consent to have this piece cut out and he'd be a sound cure. And she wouldn't write that on a paper, and the next day she left for St. John's for fear they would do it. When she got in there, he was over his operation. That was March the 20th. And February the 18th he died, the following year. Twas no one ever cured for it.

Me son only worked one month underground. He said, "I can't relish it. Dad—I sees him before me every time I turn around." So he said, "I got to come out." I got a brother that worked in '57, and he hadn't got Cancer of the lungs at all, he got Cancer of the bones. And he was only compensated this year. And I got another brother in Fortune was compensated last year. Harry Flynn and Julian Flynn. The two of them was turned down from the same thing, the mine. And me husband. And me sister's husband. Four times Harry's leg is after breaking off. It breaks off! Sat at a table in the Club, got up to have a dance, and the leg banged right off, cracked off. Went off to push up a door about a month ago and put the knee like that by the door to push off. Whanged off! They had to take him by ambulance and carry him in there. The bones was too rotten. The bones break away.

They wrote me out at 60%. I'm more than that. I got $225 a month. I got eight thousand dollars lump sum, backtime. I gets Social Assistance to make up, they give me a hundred dollars a month. Eleven youngsters in the house. Now I'm not on Social Assistance, it's only the wife and children. The Compensation looks after me drugs. I should have got more from the Compensation, because I figure I'm more than 60%. I'm not able to work, so that means I'm more than 60% disabled. If I was feeling well enough, I could go out and clean a house for somebody; I mean that's only light work. I'm not able to do that kind of stuff. I'm not able to haul nothing, or lift, not able to shovel.

I'll only live another twelve months perhaps. No one's got any guarantee, eh? I could be okay, one of the doctors told me that. If I looked after meself, you could live with the complaint that I got for a long while. But he never said what complaint it was! But I feel, I know my own feelings, that doing what I do now that I will live much longer than if I go to drink. I mean I wouldn't be able to go to a party, I wouldn't be able stand up to that kind of stuff. The way I feel now, when I gets tired, I come in and lay down for an hour or so, then I'm all right again. I see some of the guys live in the Club six days a week. Well I wouldn't be able to do that.

I never had nothing against the Company. They treated me all right, you know. I mean, they paid me for me work and that was it. They never done much for me. I had a little pension of me own built up. I got that. I was here one Christmas Eve with nothing, not a thing in the house. And I tell you what they done for me. I said, "I'll write a letter to the Company and ask for fifty dollars for Christmas." I was on thirty dollars Sick Benefit a week from the Company then, in 1969, when I first came off. So I wrote in and they sent me out a cheque for fifty dollars. And what do you think they done? Took ten dollars a week out of the thirty dollars. Honest to God! That's what the Company done for me. That's what they done for everybody.

Social Assistance, that's where the people of St. Lawrence treated rotten.

They put us on Long Term Assistance, but they had to give us Short Term while they was waiting for those papers to go through from the doctors. And when our first cheque was supposed to come in, $440, they give us $400 of Short Term. And they took the first cheque from us! Now we had to go to the dealer we were dealing with and tell him we didn't get our cheque. So he got ahold to the Welfare Officer in Marystown, and they said they took back what they paid us on Short Term. They left us a month hungry.

I'd be better treated if I only worked for the Company for a year. You wouldn't be expecting nothing then. But I mean, you work there a lifetime. I mean, I got me life work, thirty years, and that's what they done for me.

The Company used to send him a turkey or a ham every Christmas on account of he having so much service in there. And they never this year sent him so much as a Christmas card. They stopped that two years ago. No one knows why.

There's three different groups of people in St. Lawrence; the Rich, the Middle Class, and the Poor. The Rich is the big fellow, like in Salt Cove Brook. Salt Cove Brook to me today is a family circle; if you're not in that circle, you're out of luck. The Middle Class, the middle fellow, he's a bit better off than I am, the fellow is working and they're in to everything. The Poor? I'm the Poor. The poorest people, they're not looked on at all. If you're poor, you stay poor around here. They'll say plenty; they loves to speak bad of you. I wouldn't put nothing past the people of St. Lawrence today. If a strike came up tomorrow about something regarding the mines, I wouldn't even walk out with them. Every fellow's cutting the other fellow's throat. The working man's always kept down, he's looked on as nobody. And still and all, it's the working man keeping them going, eh?

I was in the Mardi Gras with the foreman's wife from Salt Cove Brook. I acted a part with her in the play. I went through practice and played it out. And so help me God, from the time I started, she never touched me. She was the Princess and I was the Maid. The foreman's wife never opened her mouth to me in three weeks. She never spoke to me cause I was the "Maid". And if they're having a party or a dance, the Middle Class, and you go in; well, there won't be three that'll speak to you.

You have to travel through it, be up against it, to raise the proof. We've got the proof, right and left, I have. I was invited out to a New Year's Ball at the Staff Club here about three years ago. I never went back no more and I never intend to. There was nothing wrong with the party, but the people were there. I went in and I was cut up. No one would let a seat to me, till one of me buddies got tired looking at me. So one of me buddies, he's a Working Class like meself but he's still working, he looked all round; every place was filled up, so he got up from his table, went and got a few chairs and invited me and her over. Only for that we would have had to leave and come home as far as the rest were concerned. They never spoke to us, never so much as to say hello. I knew every one was there, every one. I worked with them all. They knew me well, real well. No one so much as asked me how me health was getting on. So I said then, "That's it, that's St. Lawrence for you."

He made the mine! He made the first road that ever went to the mine. After working there thirty year! If there's a Time, a miner's Time going on, I don't expect we wouldn't be asked. We really would not be asked cause we're in the low class, eh? He's turned down, and we're on Social Assistance.

This is me heartbreak too. The Rich get the big thing and the Poor get the slack. You often hear on radio, all around St. Lawrence too it's on the mouth of everyone, that "you're better off on Welfare than you are working." Certainly I'm getting Compensation and part of the Social Assistance. But I can never live it down. I'm never living that down. This is me heartbreak.

10
They didn't
do their duty

VICTORIA JANES: With iron resolve and unbending discipline, this powerful widow committed the remainder of her life to her fierce ambition for her children.

I was born in Lawn. My father was born here, my mother belonged to St. Lawrence. She didn't get to school until she was fourteen; she was fourteen before she was allowed to go to school. Her mother wanted her home to spin and to do the haying and to do the work. This old man from St. Lawrence brought them over a paper, an ordinary newspaper, and my God, she looked at it and she didn't know how to read it. She said to her mother, "If this is what is going to happen to me, I may as well be blind if you don't let me go to school." So her mother let her go to school then. At that time you had to go to the A, B, C class, and she was fourteen. She was a big girl, right? But she did get on, she got to the head of the class, she did well in school. She was a very intelligent person. She could write well and she could read very well, and she could really express herself well too.

My father, he was a fisherman all his life. He could read printing, but if you wrote something in handwriting, he'd never be able to. But when he learned to read printing, my grandfather said, "That's enough, you know how to read, that's plenty, that's enough education for you to go fishing." That's all he learned.

I grew up here and of course I lived through the Depression

years. I was born in nineteen and twenty. We were poor, but I think we were happy. We always had dry fish, we had caplin, and we had our own meat. My father and my brothers shot the sea birds in the winter time and in the fall of the year. My mother used to take the livers from the cod fish and she would put them on the stove and let them render out. She used to bottle the cod oil, and we used to drink it from a spoon, she used to make us take it. I thought it was a terrible thing to do, but I realize now—I often think probably the food we had was better than they're getting now, in the deep freeze.

My father used to go in the country, and we always had oxen, not horses, and tackled them in to pull the wood. If you can see that behind the house, all that breakwater that's there, my father pulled behind the oxen. He used to bring out the sticks of cherry and she used to boil it on the stove. I often got medicine at the hospital that tasted the same thing, it was right bitter. But particularly in the spring of the year, people used to get run down, your system would get low. She used to give me that to drink; it was bitter, bitter as ever could be, but it used to pep you up. Another thing, they used to have sore hands, eh? They used to get the bark, I don't know if it was the juniper, but it was some kind of a tree, and make a poultice of it. I would say if she'd had a chance to go to school, she would have certainly been a nurse, my mother. She used to go out help people; at that time there was no hospital, but if children were being born, she'd bring clothes and wash it and bring it back to them. Very kind to people. They always found time to do the Corporeal and Spiritual Works of Mercy.

We were poor, but we had sheep. And cattle—we always had milk. My mother always knit; my mother even knit drawers for my father. The wool wasn't bought from the factory; my mother did it on a wheel. She carded it, took the wool from the sheep's back. You take the wool and you haul the wool back and forth and make it into fluffy round rolls. And you made all the rolls in the box, big balls of yarn, just as good as what I buy from Nova Scotia now. Caps, scarves, mittens, underwear, socks. You could make it fine and thick, grey or all white. My mother used to get something off the rocks, it's like a mossy stuff; they used to make a dye out of it, it used to turn the wool a different colour.

My brothers now didn't get very much education, Grade Six or

Seven. They all went fishing with my father. They had their own boat; actually, they built the boat themselves, they called it the P.J.P. It used to have a cutty on her, and when they'd go out on the Bank, they could always have a meal. They had an iron pot and they'd have a stew of fish. I had a younger sister, she died in 1958, she had her Grade Eleven, and I did.

I went teaching. I went to Roundabout. Roundabout's no longer on the map now, the people have moved. And I got $12.50 a month—remember, we're talking about nineteen and forty. And then I taught on Ellen's Island; there was no bridge there then, we used to have to go across in a dory. I had anywhere from seventeen to twenty-three children, from Grade One to Grade Eight. Now, you wanted to be a miracle worker to do anything with them. All I used to concentrate on was reading, writing and arithmetic, and of course you had to throw in religion there. But that's all you could do with them. You just had desks, chairs, probably a few pieces of chalk if you went and bought them yourself. One little blackboard and you had a sand box for some of the smaller children to play in. But that's all you had. You had no library, no reading. It was very dull. You'd have a bit of singing or you'd have a march; you had to do something to liven it up yourself. You had to use a bit of ingenuity.

Then I worked with Alcan, a filing clerk. After I got married I didn't work. He used to fish, and then he went with Alcan. When we first married, we lived with my father in that old house down there, you just see the end of it there. We came up here October the eighth, nineteen and fifty-three. So life went on from that. Nora was born in 1955; John was born in 1956; Noel was born in 1958; and Yvonne was born in 1960.

After that then, poor Jim was sick a while. '63. He was forty-three. When your X-Rays start to show up, they'll say, "Abnormality. See your Doctor." It was marked on this bit you'd get. He had had what I thought was two or three heavy colds, these chest colds. Now he always had a little Bronchitis, a heavy cough. Then he had an ulcer. Then he came up, he didn't go underground anymore, he worked on the surface. I think what gave him the ulcer, I think he worried about the X-Ray, you know what I mean? It was on his mind. Prior to this, he'd come home in the evening and if he didn't have anything to do—or even if he did—

114

he'd say to me, "Hurry up, hurry up, get me supper, I'm going to Threesticks Pond." Or, "I'm going into Gull Pond." He'd take a load on his back and he'd go fast as ever he could walk into the country, four or five miles, and he wouldn't come home until eleven or twelve o'clock in the night. When he stopped doing that, it showed me there was something . . . . My God, had to be something. That made me first think there was something.

And then it was September '64 that Dr. Hollywood sent him into St. John's. Whatever doctor he sent him into, he put him in the General on a ward with five other people. He was very upset and nervous. Friends of mine went in to see him—I had six children at home, eh?—so they phoned when they came back and they said, "My goodness, your husband is really, really, sick. He's very upset and very nervous. I think you should try to go in." Well, we never had very much money because at that time for the Sick Benefit you were only getting thirty dollars a week. But my father and father-in-law were very good to me, so I went in.

My God! Oh, he was terrible. He was very upset. He had letters there and they weren't opened, and cards. It wasn't him. I didn't know how to go about it. Mr. Jones was our Member for Burin, so I got after him, and I said I didn't think it was right; I wasn't going to leave St. John's till I saw him put somewhere different. And I didn't want him there on this ward with these people: one man had his face cut off, another man had been in an accident. It would really make you nervous yourself, looking at these people. I didn't think it was right and I think he should be put in a semi-private room at least. And they put him in a semi-private room. I didn't go in anymore then until October. He was bright and he wanted to come home. He was very sick looking and had lost a tremendous amount of weight, down to about 135 pounds from 190.

I always tried to keep the conversation interesting. Tell him about the children and what they were doing. The second time I went in, he didn't ask me about the children or anything, and that made me believe there was something radically wrong. So then I went to see Dr. Farrell: he told me what it was, Lung Cancer. That's confirmed now; I mean I knew deep in my heart what it was, right? I said, "He has faith in you now, he thinks that you are going to do something for him." "Well," he said, "you can leave

115

him here for a while, and he may get enough strength to get him home." So the first of November, 1964, his brother went in and brought him home. He came home here to the house.

Deep down I don't know if he ever convinced himself that he had Cancer. He used to say to me a few times, "When I get a bit better, you and I are going to go in to St. John's and I'm going to see a specialist." I'd say, "Yes." I knew. "We'll go in when you get better." But then the last seven or eight weeks before he died, he'd talk away to me, no sense at all. Then he'd come back to himself for a few minutes, then he'd go on again.

You know it's hard. It's only anyone in the situation can explain it. I could never bring myself—maybe I was wrong—to go in and say, "What do you want me to say to John and Noel? What do you think I should do with the children?" Maybe I was over-confident in myself that I think that, please God, I was going to be able to manage. I knew that poor Jim, God was going to take him. And I made up my mind that somehow I was going to manage. My children were going to go to school, and they were going to get educated, and they were going to go to work and make a good living for theirselves. That's the way I felt. And I knowed I had to do it. Because who was going to do it for me? No one else. And this is the path I chose.

The first few days he came home, he made two trips. One down to the meadow and he looked all around the harbour. Then he went down there. And that was the last time he was out through the door. He'd get up; he'd try to get up and he'd come out and have something to eat.

And then he got that he couldn't walk. He found it very difficult to walk. I couldn't handle him. It was very difficult for me to try to bring him around; besides, I had six children here. I didn't know how to handle a sick person. I mean some people are fit; his brother could come over, poor Jim was in bed, put his hand under him and handle him. He had this training, St. John Ambulance; but I couldn't, I only knew the one way to drag him. And he wasn't eating. So Dr. Hollywood come to a decision, and he asked Jim would he like to come in with him for a while, in the hospital. He said, "Yes, I would. I'd like to come in cause maybe you'd do something for me." So we brought him in. We brought him to the hospital on a stretcher the 22nd day of December, 1964. I went to the hospital every day, every afternoon, every after supper. I missed one night, and that night you couldn't get through the door, too stormy. But afternoon and night. Someone would come with me, my sister-in-law or his sister or someone. He'd always have somebody. He died February the 15th. But now I would say for a month or six weeks before he died, sometimes he'd sing out to a crowd he worked with. You know, he'd be saying, "Pull up the line, boy; go down and get the pump." He was living things that he used to do, working.

It's hard of course when it comes. And it does something to you. There's no way I can explain it, it's just something that you can't explain. But there were nights what I came home, and I knelt, and I asked God to take him. He was suffering, eh? It wasn't something sudden; I had myself give up to it, I was prepared. I wasn't bitter. I asked God to help me—I am a Catholic and I have faith, there's something that keeps you going. Well, I had the six children, eh? I couldn't lie down and die, could I? I had to get up and make a life for myself.

People used to come and see him, the last days at home. In the afternoon there'd be someone who didn't work; they'd come in and make the conversation general. Well, he'd perk right up, perhaps come out here and sit down, drink a cup of tea. In the night time too. Basil always came, and Rita and Peter, all our friends. I must say I never spent any time alone. That's why after poor Jim died it seemed like everyone drifted away. Only my sister and her husband used to come. And that's what I missed. I was really lonely. I used to expect these people to come when a certain time come in the night. That was hard to adjust to too. You'd be waiting for the people to come, or you'd be waiting for him to knock to say he wanted something or to do something with the children. But of course, after a while I got used to that too. I suppose the friends thought Jim was gone and I could manage. Everybody thinks, "Victoria can manage. Oh, it's all right for Victoria." So many women often say to me, "It's all right for you my dear, you're different than me, you had insurance." I had insurance, but no one ever gave it to me; I paid for it. They could have had it too.

People would say, "Are you nervous? Are you going to get someone to sleep in the house with you?" Well what in the name of God do I want anyone to sleep in the house with me? I have six children. And I came up here in 1953 and I never barred the door and the keys were in the door; and sure, I'm not going to take them out now. I never had any fears. But if I woke in the night time and I heard a sound, I got to get up and see what it is— suppose it's only a horse going up through the meadow. So that's it. No one comes in here, no matter what time they comes, but Victoria hears them. Maybe they thought, "Well, she can cope." In lots of ways I suppose I could. I must have, or I would never have survived.

New Year's Day now is very lonely. I went a couple of times with people; but this man is here with his wife, that man is here with his wife, you're by yourself. So you feel left out. Then you don't go. I went a couple of times, then I didn't go anymore. They asked me; I said no thanks, I had other invitations. But I didn't. You feel left out. Rather than feel left out, I'd stay home. These are the things sometimes that make you very lonely. But I'm not a person to dwell on things. I'd just get up and go at something else, forget about it.

When the children were small, I think it was beautiful. When John was born first, oh we were very happy. I thought that was wonderful. And when Noel too . . . when Noel was born, although he came in a hurry: All these things made me happy. Like Christmas! Oh, that was lovely; and the children were there, and the lights. And bringing them games, seeing their eyes light up, and coming in and telling you they got something for Christmas, and you knew all the time what it was. These things. And taking them when they were right small and putting parkas on them and heaving them out in the snow. We even used to go, poor Jim would cut the ice in the pond and we'd fish through the pond. He'd get a few sticks and I'd make a big fire. All these things I like to remember. You don't like to remember the sad things. Like with the children when I came home from the hospital in the night time; they'd say, "How was he?" I'd say, "Very good." I don't know whether I did right or not, but you kept your grief, you covered. You put the best side out. I brought them in a couple of times to see him, but they always made him very unhappy, and he always cried. And the Doctor said I'd better not bring them too often. It made him very lonely. So after that then I didn't bring them there; just for a minute, and then they'd go on again.

What did I do? Now this is the part. This is the part I couldn't get used to. Poor Jim worked on a dollar something an hour, and he made six thousand dollars a year. Now, I had to live on $225 a month Compensation, and I had to wait until the end of the month to get that. I didn't know how to cope with that. But poor old Jim had private Life Insurance and he had the Insurance of the Company. I used to do the best I could with that; and if I had to pay my light, and had to buy my oil, and I couldn't make it, I had to go to the Bank and draw on my savings. There was no other way. So then the Compensation gradually went up. I made my own bread. I never bought a cookie. I was home, wasn't working then. John's pants were too small; Noel wore them—the hand-me-down thing. And I was never a dresser, that never bothered me anyway.

The first year poor Jim died, the first summer, we never stayed home on Sunday. I always took the youngsters to Little Lawn, fishing and trouting. We'd go away in the hills and picnic, always went on a picnic. No matter what I had to do, I went on and brought the children. I always put my children first. I hope they turn out to make something of themselves, because I always put them first and I always put myself last. I think that's the answer. There was nothing easy about it, but when I look back I don't regret anything that I've done. I think everything was done that could be done.

But I had no inferiority complex now. I worked! I can look the world straight in the eye. I don't owe no man anything. That's my method. That's how I coped. We did all right. In '68, I went to the Bank to work part time. I mean I knew I had to do something; I wasn't going to go to some of the stores and work for seventy cents an hour, nor I wasn't scrubbing anyone else's floors, that's for sure. Bank Teller, part time, I get paid by the hour. At first, the youngsters, if I couldn't come up until six o'clock because I worked funny shifts then, they'd be all up in the window, every pane there had a face in it waiting for Mom to come home. But gradually I said to them, "Well, you'll have this done when Mom comes home this evening." And gradually the faces disappeared, and when I came home they were finished whatever. I'd tell them what to do, what to get for their supper, write it down on a note or a paper. I'd say, "I may have to work late this evening, do this,

this is in the fridge, do that, and have this for your supper." And they'd have something for me. And when I'd come home, he'd be in there doing his lessons, John'd be down there, and the other one who didn't go to school would be playing on the floor. So from that we started to adjust to only me. You know, being here with me. So that's how we survived.

The children grew up with only me. The man that did my roof last year, he's my neighbour, he calls me Aunt Vicky. "My God, Aunt Vicky," he says, "that crowd's a great hand to work with, but they don't know how to do nothing. They even hands you the hammer the wrong way." I said, "Look, they live with me, eh, and they do everything a woman's way. I don't know how to go up and put on the roof. I don't know how to put on the windows." So I often wondered, it often bothers me what effect it would have on my children. I kept very close to them and I kept watch on them, and maybe I protected them a little too much. I don't know. I just wondered if somebody who knew me and knew my children could analyse it, that's what I would like. Because it must, you know, it must have an effect somewhere.

Noel often told me things that he.... Filling out papers, your next of kin. And lots of times the boys at university, they wouldn't have any harm in it, they'd say, "And what does your old man do for a living?" Not knowing, eh? Up in school, a new teacher comes in, "What's your name? Your father's name?" You know. And one time he wouldn't say it, he was in Grade Eight; and the other crew said, "Why didn't you tell him your father was dead?" Well, he didn't want that pity, eh? I never pitied them either, nor I didn't want anyone to pity them. I did the very normal things we always done. I got up Sunday morning and we went to Mass and we came home. If it was a fine day, we packed our basket and went up on the hill. Everything as normal as I could. I didn't want anyone to say, "Poor old Victoria." I didn't want to hear that.

Making decisions was pretty hard. When John was seventeen, I had no one to say, "Should I send him to university? Should I send him down to Burin? Was he too young to go out?" I kept them very close. At half past seven they had to come in. Was I too strict? "Do your lessons, you're going for Grade eleven." Was it right, was it wrong? The decisions had to be mine and I had to do it. That I found difficult. I'd stay awake, trying to figure out will I do that. But I have this belief that if you work hard at rearing your children; if you teach your children the right things—you must respect your neighbour and your neighbour's property—that little bit of moral fibre is going to come through, no matter what they do. Maybe I'm wrong, perhaps it's something that I want to hold on to, but I'd like to believe that. I had myself believing it. I found Dr. Hollywood very helpful. If I'd ring him and ask him, I'd say, "Doctor, I want to talk to you about something." But I usually had my mind made up what I was going to do before I went. I just wanted someone to reassure me that that could be the right thing. I'd come away with the same decision that I went up; I already had it made. I can look after myself.

I have a deep concern for my children. I worry about them. If anything happened tomorrow, I'd rather for anything to happen to me, anything in the God's world than it happen to either one of them. I'd rather take it all myself, no matter what it is. I stayed with them and I encouraged them. I give them a pat on the back when they wanted it, and I give them a kick in the behind when they wanted it too. I believe in that. Not everyone could face the situation and make a better life for themselves. Some poor children, they'll never be redeemed. Their father's gone; they dropped out of school, a lot of them.

If my children were grown up and out making a good living for themselves, and they were happy and content in what they were doing, I'll think that I have accomplished something. I *have* accomplished something! I have John out, he's got his B.Sc.; Nora's a stenographer with the Department of Mines—she's got a little money saved up, she's a little bit of a miser, thank God for that; Noel's in university; Tommy's in Grade eleven, and by the way, Tommy's working four to twelve tonight in the office; and I have Leo in Grade eleven, he thinks he's going to be an engineer; Yvonne thinks she's about to go Nursing. And I think in a few year's time when I'm sixty-five, I'm going to have a valet and I'm going to enjoy my retirement. So that's Victoria!

I don't imagine myself going and living with any of my children. I wouldn't want that. I want no outlaws or in-laws because the in-laws would be outlaws after a while. So I don't want that. I don't know what I'll do. I've often thought about it. I hope I'll be able to support myself. If I don't, you can always go to Welfare.

But I don't think I'll come to that. No, I don't think so. As the children leave, my income from the Compensation is getting lower; it was $400 last year, John went off it was $350, Noel's gone off in June and now it's $300, Tommy is gone next year, it's $250.

I would never marry. In the beginning when I had the children, I don't think it can fit in. Children remember their father, and seeing someone else . . . . Perhaps I'm wrong, but that's my own idea. Of course, at my age now, who'd want me? But that never entered my mind. I'm not frowning on anyone who does this, but I could never see myself dressing for a Saturday evening, take my handbag and my money, and go over to a Club and pay my way in and sit down. Good God! I'd never never be able to do that. They do that here, the widows do that here. But when they say the word "widows," I am numbered among them. And sometimes to me that word reeks. "Widow!" Some people use it in a very scornful way; they'll say, "Oh, the widows were over to Bud's last night," meaning something was going on. Well I mean I wouldn't like to be associated with anything like that. That annoys me.

Of course Rennie Slaney's article in *The Telegram* started it all. You would think the Department of Health, or Ottawa, they would have come in. Wouldn't you? In the beginning of course they were sending them to the Sanitorium, they had "TB". You wouldn't think they had *that* much TB, my good God. Sure if you came in the home and had TB, that's passed right around. You can catch TB, pass it from one to another. They didn't do their duty. They didn't do it right.

I don't think it would ever be known only for the Doctor that did an autopsy on Isaac Slaney; and he wasn't long here before the Corporation booted him out. He left here shortly after. All suspicious minds says the Company got rid of him. I don't think anyone thought it was dust. I often heard my father say, "Their lungs is not strong enough to keep up with that, cause that's the poor times, they didn't have the food when they were growing up." That's what the older people said. They always had some kind of answer.

I suppose people didn't make enough fuss about it; no one interested enough in it to dig into it and see what it was, what was really going on. People just took it. I can't understand it when you're looking back on it. We were milder. They never got Siebert. They never got handy to him. I suppose they tried to contact him. But he's in the States, and they never got any commitment from him. To the best of my knowledge, they never got a thing from him. He made a lot of money; they had good ore up in Iron Springs, right pure, they had the best. He made a mint of money I would say. The people really should have stuck up for their rights.

11

A Company is not
a poor person,
are they?

*REBECCA FLYNN: Childless, and a widow, she
shares her tiny St. Lawrence cottage with her paraplegic brother, surrounded by a dozen other widows.*

We always looked after our stomach. Whatever we can get good to
eat, you know, the best—that's not very good what you gets
around here, I'll tell you. But now when we were on Webbers, we
had meadows, a little field of hay, and we used to keep a cow and
we had milk and butter. It was a different way coming here you
know; we left all that behind. And we had a beautiful garden. My
gracious, the cabbages I used to have. We used to go down to the
garden after Peter was home from his work, and we'd work away
at the garden—carrots and turnips and cabbage and potatoes in
abundance. And we were working hard, for of course we were
born to work hard, and we took a lot of pleasure in it, you know.
My God, I wouldn't give the past for the present, no. And we had
a horse too; I kept it for a good many year after Peter died—you
had to buy food for it, I had no way to get hay then. But it was too
much expense.

The first house my father built was a peaked roof house. Then
he built a bigger one, a two-storey home—five bedrooms upstairs,
and we had a living room and a large kitchen and a dining room.
We were a large family; we had fourteen children, seven boys and
seven girls. We had five milk cows. And they had oxen; they used

to haul wood on them—he had a horse all right, but he never liked it. They used to go away in the country and carry food enough to do them for two or three nights. You had to go further back into the country to get the logs for to build up the fishing house. That had to be done every year, you see.

We went to school. It was all right. They were very strict. The books we had then, the Carlisle Readers; you had so many blocks of spelling to learn and so many words. Education wasn't that valuable where it'd be very much use to us—only to read and write. The teacher only used to get thirty dollars a month, poor thing. The old school fell down, it got too leaky and miserable to keep. To tell the truth, mostly what I got was from the older members of the family: now they got more because they had the school, but when I come up to school, it was in Depression years. My husband, he was in the same school as I was; and when we were making our first confessions, first communions and like that, we all went together.

People had to work hard, you had to try to help your parents. We helped at everything the parents were at. If my brother went down spreading fish, well I was spreading fish, making hay and milking cows, carding wool, making yarn. You'd have the sheep and you'd take the wool from them—I can't even remember when I learned how to do those things, we were at it so young. We'd make socks and sweaters and underpants.

My father was eighty-four year old and he used to go out in the dory hisself with a few lines. And the boys used to be fishing too, Harry and Sam, and they wouldn't have left in the morning when he'd be up and gone. At nine o'clock he'd come back and he'd have a few fish off his lines; and one morning I remember his coming home with a whole dory load. Well, was he tickled. He was really active for his age. The next year the boys took the dory from him; could be he'd drop an anchor and go overboard with it, eight-four year old. He never went down to the water, what we calls the landwash, that summer to see the fish. He was right killed over it. He was all his lifetime at it.

We were never in want. Anybody that worked hard managed to get enough to feed themselves, even in Depression. Different people, it's the same now. My goodness, there's people working in that mine and they're making a fortune and they're not so well off as I am today. Different management, see? We found potatoes scarcer than flour: there'd be a boat come in the fall of the year and bring potatoes, turnips, stuff like that, and if you were able to buy enough for to do you the winter, you done that. And some poor Christians couldn't do that, they could only get so much, so they run out.

We were living in a little community with eight families, so there wasn't much recreation. We used to go to dances. My goodness, when there'd be a dance in Lawn or Lord's Cove—so between sundown and dark we were all on the road for Lord's Cove, six miles. We were allowed when we were fifteen; we had to go in care of our brothers, but we were there, and we danced all night until daylight. Keep the Time going until daylight; daylight come, back home at sunrise. No lying down in the summer time, you'd do your work. We enjoyed it. Oh my goodness that was wonderful, them Times. We done square dances. We used to have accordion and a violin. And you know it was very cheap to go to a Time; if you had a dollar it was just as good as if you had twenty-five today. There was tea, and they served food; you'd get your supper. They'd collect it all round the community, somebody's bring a cake. You'd get fifty-five, sixty articles that was sold for the Church. That's what the Times were had for, to get money for the Church.

A thing we used to have in our homes was concerts. You get up and make your part on stage, perhaps an hour and a half long. Everyone would have some little thing to do or say; dance a little dance or say a little recitation or sing a song. We used to look forward to that time of year. And then when everything would be done we'd have a couple of square sets, a dance. Oh, it was great.

When we started to go together I was seventeen and he was nineteen. But we weren't together all that time, we kind of broke off. I mean to say we weren't together all that time because of the Depression years. And I went to work for a paltry old five dollars a month in St. Pierre. I worked in St. Pierre for three years, and that's what I got, five dollars a month. My mother was living then, and in her health. The way it was them times a lot of girls used to work in St. Pierre. It was hard to get something to do and they always wanted somebody. She could speak a little English, and they didn't want me to speak French to the children—they wanted their children to learn the English. We worked hard though. They couldn't get enough of you for that paltry old five dollars they were giving you.

I came back here then and I—I used to come back every year for a month and clean up for my mother. And then I went working at the Presbytery in Lamaline, and I worked there six year in Lamaline, and then three years at the Presbytery in Burin, and then I came home to my mother. She died in March, and I was home at that until I married Peter.

I was married eight o'clock on a Friday, Old Christmas we call it. We had our plans to be married before Christmas, but the roads was blocked—snow come, oh what a snowstorm. And everything was blocked up, couldn't even get through on a horse and slide. The Priest couldn't get from St. Lawrence; it took him a whole week, the plough, to open the road. We got on horse and slide then and went up halfways and met the Priest coming and then we got in the car and went down. And we were married.

We were married in '57. We were old. I was thirty-nine and he was forty-one. I had a little difficulty when my mother died, and I was left with a paraplegic brother and my father was an old man, he was seventy-seven I guess. And I had two brothers and they were working and one brother wasn't very well. So I was, you know, more or less my own goodness I suppose, I stayed with them. I stayed with them for ten years. That's the way of things. I thought I was doing the right thing.

Then we were married. We got along together. Perhaps in the evenings we'd go up in the hills and go berry picking, go over at the hay, go walking at the beach. There was never a thing that he'd do but he'd come and tell me, get my opinion of it. There's a lot more things you understood, you know, about life, when you're married. Looking after one another and doing what we could.

Peter had been working five year in the mine then. But he didn't work steady in the mine so far as I know; he used to come out like the boys do now. You see them go fishing, and then go back again. He worked longer in the mine than he did at the fishing. Perhaps he'd come up in the spring and go fishing, and then go back in the fall. They were pretty happy with their work, and they didn't know this radiation were there. Because he said he'd never have died with it had he known it was there. He'd a never worked there. He was a young man and he didn't have to go there.

He found it all right. They had lots of hardship, because I tell you they used to have to go over the road in trucks, and lots of time they'd come off the shift at eleven or twelve o'clock but not be home till three in the morning. Before we were married he used to board there in St. Lawrence, but after that they used to come back and forth in trucks. But it was a lot of hardship.

Peter used to have a lot of those chokings then, even then. Before I was married to him, he used to tell me that he used to get out of the bed and go walking three or four times across the hall afore he could get his breath, from choking. He said it come in spurts. It was like his breath was cut off, in his throat, and he used to walk the house like that with his two fist like that; and he was strong and he'd lean on his breath as hard as he could. I don't know if you know what it sounds like, like a saw rasping through wood. And perhaps it'd be twenty minutes afore he'd get his breath back at all. He'd have these a couple times a week sometimes. After, he'd go a month, according to the weather.

He wasn't diagnosed till February, not till he was ready to die. Oftentimes he used to say, "I know I'm full of it," that's Silicosis. That's afterwards, after they come to prove it was there. He had a cousin that worked with him in the mine, and he was a driller, and he died, that man did. Now the last summer that he lived, the summer before he died, he went trapping. And Peter used to have to sit down, no breath you know, maybe three or four spells before he could come from the fishing place down there till he be home. I didn't know it, he didn't tell me about it. There was nothing else he could do. He couldn't work in the mines, he wasn't feeling that well.

It was Lung Cancer, see. You get dust first. Well, he must a had dust all those years since he got that smothering, that's when he must a got it. The Doctors never told him that's what it was. So he sat there smothering at first and he had that pain across the chest. He'd go back and forth to the Doctor and he'd give him something to help him out, that's all. They never told him what it was. Well, he used to say to hisself, that's what it is, cause he seed too much of it, see?

Well I didn't know what to think. I didn't want to let myself believe that's what it was. He went in to St. John's then in February. He said, "I'll have to go, in the name of God, it's that bad." He went down to the Doctor and the Doctor X-Rayed him and said, "Well, you'll have to go in to St. John's." They kept him in and he phoned and he said, "I've got something on my lungs." They wanted to have an operation. And he knowed that you can't be cured, because he seen too much of it. And he said, "I'm living in the midst of it Doctor, and I know what it is. But if you can tell me one that you cured, I'll be satisfied to take the operation." He said, "You can go home." And Peter said, "Yes, I can go home."

So he come home then. That was in March. He was dying from that time then, poor fellow. It was the left lung that went first, that's what the Lung Cancer took first. It was no trouble to know, that side. The feeling, you couldn't put your hand on that shoulder. I spent nights and nights up rubbing him sure. And coughing. Mother of God.

I took his bed out here in this room, where I could do a bit of work in the kitchen and I could look after him. And in the night time, round half past eleven, I'd starts getting ready for bed. And I'd give him lunch and I'd rub him with one thing and another and cross him—I mean I had faith in God, and I'd try, thinking that was going to help him. And he'd lie back for me to get in bed to go to sleep too. And the very minute his back would touch the pillow, he'd start to cough. And of course I'd be out of bed, I'd be up then, going from one place to another, getting whatever I could, a little drop of hot water, a little drop of peppermint, a little bit of Vicks, a little bit of something, just to try to feel. . . . It'd be four or five o'clock in the morning before that would let up on him. And of course I'd go to bed then, and perhaps we'd sleep till nine or ten.

He used to sit on the chesterfield there, and I tell you it was some sad. He'd say, "I'll be lonesome for you when I die." And praying. It was a hard place to work in, the mines. But you knows you're going to your death when you works there, because you knows you're going to get that radiation sooner or later. And some people got weaker lungs, I suppose, or weaker systems, and they gets it quicker. And it goes according to your age too, and the length of time you're working there. If you went there younger,

129

you're going to die younger. A cruel lot of people. There's a lot of widows in St. Lawrence.

I was worrying. Who wouldn't? I knowed it was going to come. You know, I was going to be left like this. There was never a day I suppose, never a minute, but it was flashing across your mind. The few happy years was going to end so quickly. And then again the suffering, see? You had to watch him suffering so much. I often seen him getting out of the bed and running out into the hall, trying to get his breath—so much mucous and choking up. And I'll tell you, the legs melted away, and the body. There's his picture there, when we was married. He was a healthy man.

We had a big trap skiff. Him and his brother, they jointly owned it. He'd see her going out. I was putting the stove on one morning and I heard him crying. And I went rushed into the room. I thought there was something wrong with him, and I said, "What's wrong?" Now you could see the water from here; you know where you goes out through the gulf there, and they were working up the engine there, his brother was. And he said, "My God, he's going out, and I'll never go in her again." He was breaking his heart over the old skiff. But when he mentioned anything once, he never mentioned her afterward, after he got sick. He never kept harping at anything. He was right reconciled. You never see anybody reconciled to dying before like he was. He knowed it had to come and that was it. He'd talk it over, talk over what was going to happen, what he was going to do and one thing and another. He even said one day, "If I could get well enough now for the summer, I'd get the kitchen put in here, get it changed over so you'd be handy to the other family for company for you."

But I spent the summer he died crying, out on the back door step where no one could see me. Days and days I'd go and sit down and cry till I had no tears to cry. I'd sit down to my meals and do the same thing. Twas an awful hard blow to me. We were very much in love, very happy. We never had an argument in all our lives, never any more than an "Oh dear" from him. He'd come home, he'd come in from his work from the trapping and sit down. I'd have his breakfast ready for him. "Wash me face, old woman," and I'd take a pan of water and wash him. And the same thing when he'd go out in the evening. We used to burn wood and coal and we had a space heater for the hall, and he'd go out and he'd cut up a bit of wood. He'd say, "Come out old dear, and bring in the wood for me. Don't be so lazy. Take some fat off of you." So I'd do that while he'd be cutting up the wood. Then he'd make a bit of kindling and I'd bring some water. Then he'd go out and draw some oil for the oil stove, and I'd bring the bucket of coal. And that's the way we used to live. And then when we'd get it all settled in, he'd sit down and haul off the clothes and say, "Now wash them old dear." And I'd wash them, and comb him and then we'd have a bit to eat and he'd say, "I'm going out now for a little run." And I'd lie down with a storybook, we had no TV.

When he come in from his walk he'd put his hat on the top of the cupboard. So when he was sick here in the living room he looked at it one day and he said to me, "Leave my old hat there." I left it there then and it's been up there this ten years. It's still his house. That was our life. We were never away from one another. When you have a happy life, it is a hard thing to see it broken up.

He died the 24th of June. And I was fourteen days afore he died and I never put my head, I never took off my clothes. For sleep I'd lie on the edge of the bed, cause he couldn't get into the bed, poor fellow. As soon as he touched the bed he'd cough, cough, cough. When I seen that, I couldn't leave him then. I had to stay with him. I put the bed back in the bedroom. And he sat in that chair, and I'd fold the pillows around him like at the hospital—I thought at home I could do as much for him as the hospital. I brought him home and he stayed in that chair till the day afore he died. And the day he died in the night, that morning he said, "I'd like to get into the bed." And I said, "Yes dear, we'll put you back in the bed, and if you feel uncomfortable we'll take you out." So we put him in bed, and at half past twelve, quarter to one, he died. He really wanted to get into bed to die.

He was nine days getting ready to die, with just a drop of juice. My dear, it was something to watch. I wouldn't be able to go see a miner dying. If a miner was dying, a friend of mine, I wouldn't be able to go see him. I've seen too much. You don't die with Silicosis, you *perish*. Now that's a hard thing to say, isn't it, but that's what you do. Because you know you're going to die, there's no cure for you once you gets it. You just got to wait your time to come. It was a hard, hard thing. Because you know yourself, if

131

you've got pneumonia or something, the doctor comes and gives you a needle, you're going to get better. But you get this and you know you're not going to get better. Well you wants a good heart to stand it.

The mine didn't do nothing. Never even sent him a wreath. Not one from the mine ever come to see him. I'll tell you, they never even sent a wreath. He never got Compensation until the 4th of June, and he died the 24th. We lived on our savings. Now he got his Compensation the 4th of June, and he got another cheque. They used to get paid every two weeks, that's the way the Compensation would come to him. The 18th he got another one, $86, and then the next one he got was the 4th of July. Well of course he died the 24th of June. I sent it back. They sent me back half of it.

I'm not wasting nothing. We haven't got a mansion here, it's not that big you know. It was like that when he died, it was comfortable, and I kept it that way. I looks after it the best way I can. There's lots of things I'd like to have, but I daresay I've got most of the things I need to make me comfortable. I'd like to have a nice carpet on the room, or a nice colour television. Best to forget all that. I'm happy to be living, and I don't go taking no pleasure because I'm not able. With my brother, I can't leave here, he won't stay with nobody. I never see the Bingo or nothing at all. I suppose that's the reason for the money, it's good for that. But what's the good of it if you can't get something out of life?

His nieces came to see me at Christmas, and of course the most I could talk about was their Uncle Peter. They went down and said to their mother, "My gosh, she never stops talking about him." "Yes," she said, "that's the reason they were separated, they were too happy." That's the reason he was took away from me. Some people you'll see living long lives together and they do nothing, only fight. And the happy ones, their homes are broke up. Some remarry when their husband dies, but that didn't come to me at all. I didn't want no more men once my husband was gone. He was the only man what was going to be in my life.

I don't think anybody's got anything against the Company. Well, the work was there and that was it. They didn't force them to go do it. But the Company don't do too much for the people. I think they should do something. A Company is not a poor person, are they? They get lots. And they're making plenty money from that mine now.

I wish the mine never had opened. It was a wonderful thing, St. Lawrence prosperous, Lawn too I suppose. But I tell you we had a thick graveyard, a fat graveyard. I suppose that's the way God planned it, but there's a lot of people under the sod that wouldn't be there. By God you'd see big able-bodied men, and they'd get that, and in five or six months you wouldn't know them. They were gone to a shadow.

But once your partner's gone, you don't have much of a life. Well you figure, if your wife is gone, you wouldn't have much left. You're a young man, and you might live it down, you know, after a while, and the man's different. But now when Peter died, he left me pretty comfortable. He left me no money, poor little dear, but he left me pretty comfortable in regards to the home and a bit of stuff round. And when he died, it seemed like it was all gone. I couldn't care less. It's a hard stroke, isn't it?

12
Industrial Carnage
and Social Responsibility

The quality I admire above all in human beings is the ability to surmount catastrophe. Thus it was that when I learned of the miners' agony through Ian Adams's book, *The Poverty Wall*, and talked to students at the university whose fathers, uncles, and sometimes brothers, were dead or dying, I was drawn to St. Lawrence. This attraction turned to an enraged determination when one child of the "Co-operation's" ruling elite shouted: "The miners are all faking it. They make up their diseases. No single case of Lung Cancer has ever been proved".[4]

Through one of my students I was introduced to one miner and his family, then to another. Through weekend visits I quickly developed a network of friends who were willing, even anxious, to help me expose the conditions under which the miners live and die. Once settled in Lawn for the summer, my interest and solicitude strengthened my bonds with the sick miners and widows, my personal expertise with gun and darts cemented sporting alliances with the younger men, and through them to their fathers.

If the people were suspicious of "the Professor", they showed no sign of it. Time after time they welcomed me into their homes with that warmth and cordiality which is Newfoundland's hallmark. With but little encouragement they told the stories of their lives with the verbal eloquence which is Newfoundland's genius. Most told me what a relief it was for them to release their grief and despair—and in the same process, give meaning to their torment.

[4] In fact, the Royal Commission and a series of scientific publications together clearly established cause and effect in the 1960s.

Nothing can be gained by pretending the work was a pleasure for me. It was not. It was terribly depressing. It is one thing to read a disembodied account in a book; quite another thing to hear it first hand from the man himself—sometimes kneeling over a chair on the floor beside you, always gasping for breath.

Throughout that summer of 1974 I stumbled from house to house, tape recorder and notebook in hand, trying to catch the men on days when the weather was neither so fine that they left their homes for the clubs and stages, nor so bad that their lungs congested and blocked so they could not spare the breath for speech.

In the second week of my stay my spirit was shattered by the only hostility directed towards my work that summer—from an outraged girl who had lost her father and three uncles to the mine disease. With the angry despair that grips so many of her generation of Laurentians and Lawners, she berated me for forcing her widowed mother to relive her agony—"She'll cry herself to sleep for two weeks now you've raked it all up again. And it'll all be for nothing. Nobody can do anything." Devastated by this encounter, terrified that her cynicism might be far more accurate than my own optimistic cliches—that it would all be for nothing—I almost abandoned the book. It was only the arrival a few days later of a letter from a colleague at Memorial (to whom I had sent a draft of Becky Flynn's autobiography) saying that I had set my hand "to a noble task" which gave me the courage to go on.

But the young girl had much truth to tell. This book *must* have some practical consequence. If it does not, it is nothing more than some obscene pornography of death.

Why are the men of St. Lawrence and their ten hundred thousand fellows throughout the industrial world left to die in squalor and bitterness, their physical suffering compounded by their fear for their families' future? As he slowly chokes to death, why must Pat Sullivan's last years be filled with the sights and sounds of his son's more ghastly ordeal? Why must Harry Andrews spend his last years on his knees on the floor when hospital-designed equipment might alleviate his suffering? Why was Alphonse Reilly not given the dignity of a small shop in which to exercise his talents during his remaining years? On what grounds does Sammy Byrne, at 46, receive seventy-five dollars a month as total recompense for

135

his impending death? Why are there no social facilities to provide human contact and the comfort of communion with his fellows for Alonzo Malraux? Why are there no strong young men paid to lift the miners, and buses to carry them from home to Social Centre? Why must Paul Duff die with only the memory of his humiliation in his treatment as a "Welfare Person"? Why was Becky Flynn's Compensation cut off the day her husband breathed his last? These terrible wrongs must be ameliorated by compassionate legislation.

From the time this manuscript leaves my hands until it reaches its first readers, two of the co-authors of this volume will probably have died and two of their neighbours (who mined in the pre-Alcan days) have developed new cases of Lung Cancer or Silicosis. In that same time, an estimated *half million men and women*[5] around the world will have died from industrial accident and disease. Countless hundreds of thousands more will have been maimed and disabled. This unforgiveable toll will continue each year until industrial nations are forced to address themselves to these problems. Nowhere is the moral bankruptcy of industrial society better documented than in its industries' death roll and in its governments' pitiful attempts at "compensation".

The scale of this carnage constitutes a holocaust. Yet the attention it has received from scholars and journalists, medical and public officials, has been disturbingly minimal. I do not believe myself to be over-stating the case in saying that this neglect constitutes, at best, criminal incompetence; at worst, a conspiracy to withhold information and deny all reasonable succour.

* * *

In the ten autobiographies printed in this book I have tried very hard to avoid singling out the obvious villains of the piece. To this end I have excised from the transcriptions many pejorative accounts of the behaviour of individuals and institutions, corporations and government departments. Nevertheless, some private

---

[5] How many? No one can say with any certainty for records are rarely kept and still more rarely released—and medical knowledge is incomplete. This estimate of one half million deaths is a crude extrapolation of the American figures of 100,000 dead per year.

individuals and some public institutions have been seen in a most unfavourable light. In some of these cases guilt is apparent. In others—especially that of the Compensation Board, the Welfare Officers, Alcan, and some members of the medical profession—blame has been apportioned too heavily, for these individuals are the only enemies visible to the dying men and their families. In fact, most people working on behalf of the compensation, welfare and medical agencies have behaved with as much sensitivity and compassion as most people can summon; and Alcan merely inherited the problems of the "Co-operation". I introduce these strictures here out of a profound wish that any anger generated by the ten autobiographies in this volume be put to some useful purpose.

For while this book has focused narrowly on one continuing disaster in a few isolated Canadian communities, the problem is truly an international one. Neither industrial carnage nor stunningly inadequate compensation are exclusively Canadian problems (indeed, Canada's handling of this problem is less inadequate than many other industrial nations). If the point is not fully grasped that this is an international problem, then the personal anguish that so many hundreds of thousands have suffered will have been for naught.

The autobiographies which appear in this book must be seen in a wider perspective as but one chapter in a world-wide tragedy which links the dead and dying miners of Canada with their American, British, Japanese, Belgian and South African counterparts— all devastated by innumerable diseases and catastrophes; the 100,000 deaths and 390,000 disabling diseases caused each year by industry in the U.S.A. alone (1972, "President's Report on Occupational Safety and Health"); the 50,000 French men and women who are "handicapped" each year by industrial accidents. Nowhere is the scale of this tragedy better outlined than in Rachel Scott's *Muscle and Blood:*

> We have worshipped progress and profits, made gods of science and industry, blindly ignoring the evidence around us that they were destroying us. Workers die daily in explosions and fires, are mangled by machinery, deafened by industrial clangor, and driven to the breaking point by harassment and the command to work at a dangerous pace. Hundreds of

thousands of men and women are poisoned at work by fumes and solvents and suffocated by lung-filling dusts. Yet, ignorant as primitive tribesmen of the human results of a burgeoning technology, most of them die quietly, their families accepting deceptive diagnoses. . . . "

For too long this terrible death toll has gone unrecognised. Moreover, it is all too clear that this blindness is no accident, but a function of what the Association of Trial Lawyers of America has called the "total callousness, stupidity and deceit of the medical-industrial complex consisting of company doctors, industry consultants, and key occupational-health officials."

* * *

It is now all too apparent that the "mass luxury" of modern industrial society is nothing but a sham, an illusion built upon the concealed death and suffering of uncounted millions. With this knowledge in hand, it is incumbent upon all industrial nations to re-assess the extent and scope of their obligations to the men and women whose work creates real wealth. This reassessment must concentrate on at least two major areas.

The first is a re-thinking of the *political economy* of industrial production. At present, politico-economic forces dictate that resources be exploited and goods produced at minimum expense and without serious regard for the hazards encountered by labour. Now that the true social and personal costs of this system are beginning to be understood, no civilised society can seriously contemplate its maintenance. The barest humane response demands a political economy which prohibits all production which cannot be made safe.

Each nation must enact strong legislation and create national agencies with the power to enforce this legislation; and this power must be on a level with national police forces, not buried in the castrated civil service. Genuinely independent research must be initiated immediately into the disease and accident rates of different industries and companies, and the major offenders halted until appropriate measures are determined and executed.

If goods or material cannot be produced under the present technology with a major reduction of disease, then science must develop a new technology: if it cannot, then production of that material must be abandoned.

Secondly, all our notions of what constitutes just *compensation* must be re-assessed, for there has been virtually no change in this since the 19th Century. Since the initial German legislation was passed in the 1880s and copied elsewhere in the industrial world, the problem has been regarded as largely solved. Indeed, a recent scholarly work has been able to announce with some satisfaction that while "before 1897 the injured worker found himself in severe difficulty . . . today he may resort to national health service for his medical treatment, state-administered workmen's compensation while incapacitated and Unemployment Insurance to tide him over between jobs".[6]

In fact, however, Compensation is normally geared either to comparable Welfare benefits or to some arbitrary proportion of the workman's former wage: the former is an affront to the dignity of men and women who have worked all their lives; the latter is unacceptable under the best of circumstances (the full salary was rarely enough) and is now made laughable by the process of inflation. Whatever the principle a country may use in the calculation of compensation, the normal consequence is that the dying or disabled workman finds himself and his family reduced to the stature of those who cling to Welfare. When he dies, his family will enter that endless Welfare cycle of dependence and humiliation which continues for generations.

The stunning inadequacy of international systems of Compensation is particulary apparent in communities such as St. Lawrence which have been devastated by large-scale disasters. When the barest humanity demands massive transfusions of public monies for social, psychiatric and medical facilities, there is only a meagre individual allotment.

In this book I have used the anthropological technique of the life history to illuminate the personal dimensions of industrial carnage. But this illumination must have some purpose, and that must be a total reassessment of our notions of obligation and responsibility. There can be no better time than now, with the current

[6] Hanes, David. The First British Workmen's Compensation Act, 1897. New Haven: Yale University Press, 1968.

inflationary state of the world economy, to revalue the costs of all goods and services on a scale consonant with the hazards endured in their production. Neither can there be any better time to begin the intensive policing of our industries and the abrupt cessation of work whose hazards cannot be reduced.

Undoubtedly these proposals will be met with the same distaste that has greeted all social legislation since the 19th Century—that it will "destroy industry", that it "interferes with man's freedom", that it is a "challenge to free enterprise". But such legislation is none of these things. It is the minimum recompense that a civilisation must offer its victims.

Epilogue

In the spring of 1977, Alcan began hinting that it intended to close the St. Lawrence mines—not because they were not making a profit from them, but because they found an even more profitable supply in Mexico. In the distressing scenes that followed, the protests of the local community and the provincial government were brushed aside. My own letters and telegrams produced nothing but insipid responses from Ottawa: the Hon. Don Jamieson, Secretary of State and M.P. for St. Lawrence, expressed horror at doing anything punitive against Alcan that might "jeopardize jobs at other Alcan locations across Canada"; and the Prime Minister referred my correspondence to his colleagues, all of whom regretted that nothing could be done. One of the Prime Minister's aides confided to me that they saw no point in taking drastic action, since there were so few voters in St. Lawrence. On the 31st of January, 1978, Alcan made good on its promise and closed the mine for all time, flooding the shafts, and leaving behind only three security guards to mind their possessions. With Alcan's departure, the community's economic life died, and the younger people began their exodus to mainland Canada.

Dying Hard has had a great commercial and critical success: but reports reach me from time to time observing that the rich and cherished middle class students of central Canada do not believe that such a thing has occurred in their own country. In their innocent ignorance they reflect what seems to be the dominant Canadian will—to sweep St. Lawrence under the carpet, deny its past, and ignore its present.

141

References

I am very grateful to David Alexander, Rex Clark, Dennis Happy, Keith Matthews, and David Strong for providing me with unpublished information which I was able to use in chapters one and twelve. In addition, I found the following published works useful:

Adams, Ian. 1970. *The Poverty Wall.*
  Toronto: McClelland and Stewart.
Brodeur, Paul. 1974. *Expendable Americans.*
  New York: The Viking Press.
de Villiers, A. J. and J. P. Windish. 1964. "Lung Cancer in a
  Fluorspar Mining Community: I." *British Journal of Industrial
  Medicine,* 21: 94-109.
Hanes, David. 1968. *The First British Workmen's Compensation
  Act, 1897.* New Haven: Yale University Press.
Parsons, W. D., et al. "Lung Cancer in a Fluorspar Mining
  Community: II." *British Journal of Industrial Medicine,* 21:
  110-116.
Report of Royal Commission Respecting Radiation,
  Compensation and Safety at the Fluorspar Mines, St.
  Lawrence, Newfoundland. 1969.
Scott, Rachel. 1974. *Muscle and Blood.*
  New York: E. P. Dutton.
Slaney, Rennie. 1969. Ms. quoted in Royal Commission.